Cover Image Credit/Copyright Attribution: IIIerlok_Xolms/Shutterstock

The Paradox of Gendarmeries:
Between Expansion, Demilitarization and Dissolution

Derek Lutterbeck

Published by
Ubiquity Press Ltd.
6 Osborn Street, Unit 2N
London E1 6TD

First published 2013

Editors: Alan Bryden & Heiner Hänggi
Production: Yury Korobovsky
Copy editor: Cherry Ekins

DOI: https://doi.org/10.5334/bbs

This book was originally published by the Geneva Centre for the Democratic Control of Armed Forces (DCAF), an international foundation whose mission is to assist the international community in pursuing good governance and reform of the security sector. The title transferred to Ubiquity Press when the series moved to an open access platform. The full text of this book was peer reviewed according to the original publisher's policy at the time. The original ISBN for this title was 978-92-9222-286-4.

SSR Papers is a flagship DCAF publication series intended to contribute innovative thinking on important themes and approaches relating to security sector reform (SSR) in the broader context of security sector governance (SSG). Papers provide original and provocative analysis on topics that are directly linked to the challenges of a governance-driven security sector reform agenda. SSR Papers are intended for researchers, policy-makers and practitioners involved in this field.

The views expressed are those of the author(s) alone and do not in any way reflect the views of the institutions referred to or represented within this paper.

Suggested citation:
Lutterbeck, D. 2018. *The Paradox of Gendarmeries: Between Expansion, Demilitarization and Dissolution.* London: Ubiquity Press. DOI: https://doi.org/10.5334/bbs. License: CC-BY 4.0

Contents

INTRODUCTION

Over the past two decades the evolution of the security landscape in Western Europe (and elsewhere) has been characterized by an increasing blurring of internal and external security. Many contemporary security challenges – such as international terrorism and transnational organized crime – no longer neatly fit into one category, as they typically have both internal and external dimensions. For security institutions, especially the police and the military, this means that their roles have increasingly converged, for example with military forces becoming more involved in domestic security, or traditionally domestic security forces, such as the police, playing an increasingly prominent role at the international level.[1]

A noteworthy aspect of this convergence of internal and external agendas is the growing importance of security agencies, such as gendarmerie-type forces, that are located at the traditional intersection between domestic and international security. Thus in 2004 this author, for example, pointed to a "rise of gendarmeries" as a distinctive feature of the post-Cold War security landscape, and a number of other security analysts have made similar arguments in recent years.[2] Evidence of this development is seen in the considerable expansion of gendarmerie-type forces since the 1990s, as well as their increasingly important role in addressing many security challenges of the contemporary period, ranging from border control and counterterrorism to international peace operations.

Yet developments that seem to contradict the apparent rise of gendarmeries can also be observed. In many, if not all, European countries with gendarmerie-type forces, there have been calls for the demilitarization or "civilianization" of these forces, implying a change in their military character to bring them closer to "ordinary" or civilian-style police. In some countries, notably Austria and Belgium, this development has gone as far as to result in the dissolution of the gendarmeries and their integration into the civilian police.

The aim of this paper is to analyse these seemingly contradictory developments by comparing the evolution of gendarmerie-type forces over the last three decades in both Western and non-Western countries. Using examples from Europe, the Middle East and North Africa allows for a description of how the gendarmerie model functions in differing social and political contexts. More specifically, this paper seeks to address four questions.

- How have gendarmeries changed over the last three decades in terms of their functions, institutional characteristics and human and material resources?
- What have been the rationales behind maintaining, demilitarizing or dissolving gendarmerie-type forces in these different contexts?
- What are the main factors that have led to change among gendarmeries, and how are these forces likely to evolve in the future?
- What is the added value of gendarmerie-type forces *vis-à-vis* a clear-cut split between military and police, and external and internal security functions?

The remainder of this introductory section discusses the definition of the term "gendarmeries", provides a brief historical background to their emergence and describes their main characteristics and tasks. This is followed by an account of the expansion of gendarmerie-type forces in Europe over the last three decades in terms of both manpower and functions. The paper then turns to the institutional evolution of the three most important gendarmerie forces in Europe – the French Gendarmerie, the Italian Carabinieri and the Spanish Guardia Civil – highlighting current reform debates and in particular the question of their "demilitarization". In the next section the cases of Austria and Belgium, where the gendarmeries have been demilitarized and subsequently dissolved, are discussed. The final empirical section describes the nature and functions of gendarmerie forces in Algeria,

Morocco, Tunisia and Turkey, in order to provide examples of the evolution of gendarmeries outside the European context.

Having documented the seemingly contradictory developments towards, on the one hand, the growing importance of gendarmeries, and on the other hand increasing calls for their demilitarization or even dissolution, an explanation is offered with reference to two broad and at least partly opposing historical trends: the demilitarization or "civilianization" of internal security, and the convergence of internal and external security agendas. The influence of these larger trends is set against the backdrop of domestic political conditions to explain how the character of gendarmerie-type forces varies between the countries and regions examined.

What is a gendarmerie?

A considerable challenge in analysing gendarmerie-type forces is that there is no universally accepted definition of the term "gendarmerie", nor a standard description of such a force – even though the French Gendarmerie served as a model for many of these agencies. Moreover, other terms, such "paramilitary" or "constabulary" forces, are often used by analysts in this context, sometimes confusing more than they clarify.[3]

Generally speaking, within the existing literature it is possible to distinguish between a narrower definition of the term, focusing on military status, and a broader definition of "gendarmerie", focusing on military characteristics. According to the narrow definition, a gendarmerie is a police force with a formal military status, and which is at least partly answerable to the ministry of defence. In Western Europe this applies, for example, to the French Gendarmerie, the Italian Carabinieri and the Spanish Guardia Civil. All these examples are police forces with military status, meaning their officers have the legal status of soldiers. Moreover, these forces are, at least in certain respects, controlled by ministries of defence, although they may also be answerable to other ministries (usually the interior ministry), depending on their mission or the specific details of their legal status.

However, a somewhat broader use of the term "gendarmerie" focuses on the military characteristics of a police organization rather than its formal status as military or civilian. From this perspective, any police force with certain military characteristics relating to organizational structure, institutional affiliation, doctrine or weaponry, for example, could be considered a gendarmerie, even without having formal military status.[4] In Western Europe this broader definition would cover agencies such as the (now dissolved) Austrian Federal Gendarmerie and the German Federal (Border) Police, both of which have (or had) certain military characteristics in terms of structure and weaponry, and also used to have formal military status but have over time been demilitarized and brought under the exclusive control of the interior ministry.

While this paper does not take a definitive stance on these definitional issues, the analysis will centre on forces that fall under the narrow definition of gendarmerie, i.e. police forces with formal military status. From this perspective, the analysis will show how increased demand for deployment of gendarmeries in addressing several contemporary security challenges as well as trends towards their demilitarization and even dissolution are changing the status, character and missions of gendarmerie forces in different contexts.

Emergence, characteristics and functions

Without going into a detailed history, it can be noted that the first gendarmerie in the modern sense developed in France during the time of the French Revolution. In 1791 the French Gendarmerie (Gendarmerie nationale) was created on the basis of the so-called Maréchaussée, which had origins dating back to the pre-modern or even late mediaeval period. In the course of the nineteenth century similar gendarmerie forces were set up in a number of other countries in Europe and beyond, as a result of either direct or indirect French influence. Outside the European context, gendarmeries were introduced in most if not all former French colonies (especially those in Africa), and a number of countries which did not fall under French control, such as Turkey and several Latin American countries, also followed the French police model.[5]

The distinctive feature of gendarmerie forces is that they were composed of military personnel, but their principal task was to maintain law and order in the interior, mostly in rural areas, and along major thoroughfares. In the context of consolidating European statehood, gendarmeries were essentially instruments of the central powers in extending and strengthening their rule over the national territory, in particular the often "unruly" countryside. As such, one of their main tasks was to deal with particularly severe forms of internal strife and turmoil, which in many European countries accompanied the nation-building process.[6] Beyond their role in internal security, gendarmerie forces have also regularly been deployed in external security roles during inter-state conflicts. The French Gendarmerie, for instance, actively participated in all of France's major wars, both as military police and as a combat force.

While gendarmerie-type forces can be found in many parts of the world, including Africa, Latin America and the Middle East, among Western industrialized countries they are typically a feature of continental European states and at least formally did not develop in Anglo-Saxon or Scandinavian countries.[7]

Despite the considerable differences between gendarmeries, even under the narrow definition of the term, it can be argued that their military status is typically reflected in the following features. In terms of internal structure, they are organized along military lines, and are thus more centralized and hierarchical than "ordinary", i.e. civilian-style, police forces. They are usually equipped with heavier weaponry and equipment, including stronger suppression capabilities than is common for purely civilian police, such as armoured vehicles, small airplanes, helicopters and light infantry weapons. Moreover, gendarmeries are typically controlled (in most respects) by the defence ministry, even if they might also be answerable to other ministries, such as the interior or justice ministry.

The military status of gendarmeries often has implications for human resources that further differentiate gendarmerie personnel from civilian police officers. As soldiers, gendarmerie officers usually do not have the right to go on strike or join unions, and they are also obliged to be "permanently available", i.e. they do not have fixed working hours. They are often housed in lodgings provided by the state – usually military barracks – and thus do not live among the civilian population, as would be the case for regular police.

In terms of function, the typical tasks of gendarmerie-type forces could in principle include any aspect of policing or law enforcement, and it is therefore difficult to distinguish any general characteristics of gendarmeries on this basis. In countries following the French model of a dual police system at the national level, gendarmeries are typically responsible for policing rural areas, where they perform practically the entire spectrum of law enforcement functions. Where responsibilities are not based on geographical criteria alone, they are often defined thematically. Thus gendarmeries tend to be used for dealing with particularly serious internal disturbances that may call for a more robust response than ordinary (i.e. civilian-style) police forces are able to provide. This usually includes fighting terrorism and serious forms of organized crime, and riot control, for example. Moreover, even though the main functions of gendarmeries are in the field of internal security and policing, they often also have a (subsidiary) military defence function, which they would assume in the event of war – again a reflection of their military status.

Arguments for and against gendarmerie-type forces

While regular armies and civilian police forces are commonly accepted as essential elements of a state's coercive apparatus, the rationale for gendarmerie-type forces is more contested. Critics of gendarmeries typically see them as anachronistic institutions representing the militarization of internal security. They argue that, in a liberal-democratic state, law enforcement and internal security activities should be carried out by civilian police forces only, and view the use of semi-military forces in a police function as incompatible with civil liberties and democratic principles. To illustrate this point, critics often refer to the use of gendarmeries by former authoritarian regimes in Europe, where such forces often served as the main instruments of internal repression, such as the Spanish Guardia Civil under Franco and the Italian Carabinieri under Mussolini. According to this view, gendarmerie forces should be either demilitarized, i.e. their military status should be removed, or dissolved and merged with the civilian police.

While such criticism is not uncommon – even if traditionally coming mainly from the left wing of the political spectrum – it should be noted that there is currently no generally accepted or legally binding norm at the European level which stipulates that police forces should be civilian in nature rather than military. The European Police Code of Ethics, for example, which was adopted by the Council of Europe in 2001, states that police forces "shall be under the responsibility of civilian authorities" (Article 13), but remains silent as to the status of a country's police as either military or civilian. Thus while there is some consensus, at least in the European context, as to the imperative of civilian control over police forces, this does not extend so far as to require that the forces themselves be civilian in nature.

Nevertheless, there is at least one significant, pan-European organization that has advocated the civilian status of police forces, namely the European Confederation of Police (EuroCOP), an umbrella organization of 35 national police unions from across Europe.[8] Article 2 of the EuroCOP Statute defines a police service as a "civil, democratically controlled public body". In line with this provision, EuroCOP has called for the demilitarization of European police forces with military status. Indeed, the demilitarization of the Spanish Guardia Civil, which is the only gendarmerie force represented within the organization, has been a particular focus of EuroCOP's activities.

Yet there are also arguments in favour of gendarmeries. In countries that have such forces, at least two justifications are typically evoked.[9] First, it is argued that the intermediary status of gendarmeries makes them important, even indispensable, in bridging the gap between domestic and international security. Given that many contemporary security challenges defy the distinction between domestic and international, having a security force that combines both police and military characteristics is considered a significant asset.[10] Second, the argument is made that having two, or more, separate police forces at the national level prevents the (over)centralization of the security apparatus, and thus better protects civil liberties.[11] This argument may find less traction in federally structured states, because deconcentration of police power can also be achieved by devolving authority over the police from the federal to the state level – as for example in the USA, Germany or Switzerland. In contrast, for politically centralized states, having police forces with different statuses – i.e. civilian and military – attached to different ministries acts as a mechanism of "checks and balances" against the abuse of power. Thus while the critics of gendarmeries often see these forces as a potential threat to civil liberties, somewhat paradoxically their proponents view gendarmeries as offering better protection for individual freedoms under a dual system composed of both a military and a civilian police force, compared to a single civilian force.

THE RISE OF GENDARMERIES IN EUROPE

At least two broad developments over the last three decades seem to point to a "rise" or growing importance of gendarmerie-type forces in Western European countries: firstly, these agencies have expanded more than other security forces, and secondly, they have come to play an increasingly prominent role in addressing many security challenges of the post-Cold War period.

Expanding in size

Looking first at the simple expansion in size of European gendarmeries over the last three decades, Table 1 on page 14 compares growth in personnel numbers within gendarmeries and regular armed forces across those European countries which have (or had) such agencies. Calculating the overall average for both types of security forces reveals that, while the manpower of the regular military contracted on average by around 40 per cent between 1980 and 2010, gendarmerie-type agencies expanded by around 30 per cent over the same period.

If this table shows that gendarmeries have gained in relative importance *vis-à-vis* conventional armed forces, a lack of systematic data prevents a similar observation regarding the position of gendarmerie-type forces relative to "ordinary" (i.e. civilian) police forces.[12] However, available information does suggest that while regular police forces have also expanded over recent decades, they have not grown as much as gendarmeries, possibly

Table 1: Personnel numbers for regular military and gendarmerie-type forces in Western European countries, 1980–2010

		1980	1990	2000	2010
Austria	Armed forces	50,300	42,500	35,500	34,900
	Gendarmerie	11,000	11,794	15,751	Disbanded
Belgium	Armed forces	87,900	92,000	39,250	38,844
	Gendarmerie	16,300	16,800	Disbanded	Disbanded
France	Armed forces	494,730	461,250	294,430	238,591
	Gendarmerie	78,000	91,800	94,950	103,376
Germany	Armed forces	495,000	469,000	321,000	244,324
	Federal (Border) Police	23,564	25,187	39,240	41,000
Greece	Armed forces	181,500	162,500	159,170	156,600
	National Guard	26,000	26,500	34,000	34,500
Italy	Armed forces	366,000	389,600	250,600	292,983
	Carabinieri	84,000	111,400	110,000	107,967
	Guardia di Finanza	52,150	52,280	66,983	61,286
Netherlands	Armed forces	114,980	102,600	51,940	40,537
	Mauréchausée	3,900	4,700	5,200	5,953
Portugal	Armed forces	59,540	68,000	44,650	42,910
	Republican Guard	13,000	19,000	25,300	26,100
Spain	Armed forces	342,000	274,500	166,050	221,750
	Guardia Civil	64,000	63,000	75,000	72,600

Sources: Various years from annual publications: International Institute for Strategic Studies, *Military Balance* (London: IISS, 1981, 1991, 2001 and 2011); Guardia di Finanza, *Rapporto Annuale* (Rome: Guardia di Finanza, 1981, 1991, 2001 and 2011); Derek Lutterbeck, "Between Police and Military: The New Security Agenda and the Rise of Gendarmeries", *Cooperation and Conflict*, 39(1), 2004, pp. 45–68.

with some exceptions. In France, for example, the Gendarmerie grew by 25 per cent between 1980 and 2010, whereas the country's other police force at the national level, the Police Nationale, grew only by around 14 per cent over this period.[13] In Austria the Federal Gendarmerie also expanded by around 25 per cent between 1980 and 2000 (although it was dissolved in 2005), whereas the size of the Federal Police (Bundespolizei) remained constant during the same period.[14] In a similar pattern, the size of the Spanish National Police remained practically constant between 1990 and 2010, compared to an expansion of 13 per cent in the Guardia Civil.[15]

The reason for this growth of gendarmerie forces may of course have a number of contributing factors, including population increases in the zones of gendarmerie responsibility (as in France) or the adoption of new laws and regulations which enhance the need for law enforcement operations. Moreover, as society becomes more complex, so do the technical and scientific requirements of police work, which in turn might drive the growth of law enforcement agencies. However, the main point here is that among the major security forces of Western European countries – i.e. the regular military, the gendarmerie and the civilian police – it is the "intermediary" force that in many (or most) cases has expanded the most over recent decades, reflecting the growing importance attached to such agencies compared to both the regular military and the civilian police.

Expanding in scope

As significant as this expansion in relative manpower within European gendarmeries are the new or expanded roles and missions they have taken on. Over recent years gendarmerie-type forces have come to assume an increasingly prominent role in addressing a number of key security challenges of the post-Cold War period, ranging from areas such as border control, counterterrorism and riot control to international peace operations. The following discusses each of these roles separately.

Gendarmeries in border control

Many gendarmeries forces of European countries have become increasingly involved in border and immigration control efforts, in a response to the growing concern in recent years with irregular immigration and cross-border crime in almost all EU countries. Thus a common trend since the early 1990s has seen gendarmeries increasingly mobilized in border enforcement operations, especially along the outer borders of the EU or Schengen area, with many of these agencies undergoing a dramatic expansion as a result. Arguably the most striking example of this trend has been the (former) German Federal Border Police (Bundesgrenzschutz – BGS), whose staff rose by more than 60 per cent in a decade, increasing from 25,000 in 1990 to almost 40,000 in 2000, while the BGS budget almost tripled over the same period, from €1.3bn to €3.2bn.[16] And in other European countries gendarmerie-type forces involved in border control have grown impressively in an effort to prevent irregular migration and cross-border crime from outside the EU. In Italy, for example, the Finance Guard (Guardia di Finanza), which has traditionally been responsible for controlling the country's maritime borders, saw its personnel grow from about 52,000 to more than 66,000 officers, while its budget increased from €1.21bn to €3.21bn between 1990 and 2000.[17] Similarly, the Spanish Guardia Civil, whose remit also includes controlling the country's borders, expanded from 63,000 to 75,000 officers and its budget from €1.26bn to €1.86bn over this period.[18]

The fact that gendarmerie-type forces, as opposed to civilian-style police, now play a predominant role in border and immigration control is, at least to some extent, due to their hybrid nature and the heavier equipment at their disposal. In particular the task of monitoring "green" (i.e. land) and "blue" (i.e. sea) borders requires assets that civilian police forces typically do not have, such as airplanes, helicopters and oceangoing patrol boats. Moreover, the centralized and hierarchical structure of gendarmeries – a typical feature of military organization – may make them more suitable for operating over the vast and open spaces involved in border control.[19] And this dynamic also works in the opposite direction: as a result of their increasing deployment in border control, gendarmeries have generally been equipped with more heavy equipment thought fit to this mission. Thus between 1990 and 2000 alone the fleet of the aforementioned Italian Guardia di Finanza expanded from 330 to almost 600 boats. Similarly, the Spanish Guardia Civil saw its number of patrol boats rise from fewer than 20 in 1995 to more than 70 in 2010.[20] Indeed, it is the increasing deployment and expansion of this type of militarized approach to border control by gendarmerie-type agencies that has often been decried by human rights and migrant support organizations as an unacceptable "militarization" of the EU's outer borders and the construction of a "fortress Europe".

Gendarmeries in counterterrorism

Combating terrorism has traditionally been one of the principal tasks of gendarmerie-type forces. Most, if not all, European gendarmeries have specialized counterterror units, many of which were created following the terrorist assassinations of Israeli athletes at the 1972 Olympic Games in Munich, and the concern with terrorism more generally that this event

                    Derek Lutterbeck

triggered. Examples of such counterterror gendarmerie units include the Groupement d'Intervention (GIGN) of the French Gendarmerie, the GSG 9 (formerly Grenzschutzgruppe 9) of the German Federal (Border) Police, the Gruppo Intervento Speciale (GIS) of the Italian Carabinieri and the EKO Cobra (formerly Gendarmerieeinsatzkommando) of the now defunct Austrian Federal Gendarmerie. These are all elite police forces that are trained and equipped to deal with particularly dangerous criminals.

Data on these typically highly secretive units are difficult to come by, but the available information indicates they have expanded continuously over recent decades, even though these forces remain by their nature very small. Thus since their inception in the 1970s, the French GIGN has expanded from fewer than 100 to some 400 agents,[21] the German GSG 9 from 180 to also around 400[22] and the EKO Cobra of the former Austrian Federal Gendarmerie from 100 to 450 officers.[23]

The growing counterterrorism role of gendarmerie forces has expressed itself in an increasing number of counterterror missions, where gendarmeries have often been deployed jointly with the armed forces. The French Gendarmerie, for example, has been mobilized regularly in recent years under the Vigipirate programme. This is a counterterror operation that was launched for the first time in 1995 in response to the Paris Metro bombings carried out by members of the Armed Islamic Group (GIA) in the context of the Algerian civil war. The objective of Vigipirate is to protect certain sensitive sites and installations, such as the transport system, airports and nuclear installations, against potential terrorist attacks. Similarly, the Italian Carabinieri has taken part, often jointly with the Italian armed forces, in a number of counterterror operations on national territory in recent years.[24]

Gendarmeries in riot control

A further area where gendarmeries have come to play an increasingly significant role is riot control and protest policing. In most Western industrialized countries protest movements have become more prevalent over recent decades, and have also come to be viewed by state authorities as a growing challenge to public order. Since the anti-nuclear movements of the 1950s and the anti-Vietnam War and student protests of the late 1960s and early 1970s, protest movements are generally considered to have become much better organized, more powerful and more socially diverse.[25]

The principal reason why riots and mass protests led by such movements are now met mainly by gendarmerie-type and not civilian police forces can, again, be seen in their centralized structure and their ability to operate in larger formations – aspects often considered essential in the policing of mass demonstrations. Indeed, prior to the twentieth century in most European countries it was not uncommon for governments to deploy regular armed forces in the event of large-scale riots and protests. It was only during the course of the twentieth century that this task was increasingly assumed by specialized police, and in particular gendarmerie-type forces, as the use of the armed forces for controlling riots and demonstrations came to be seen as an inappropriate tactic in conflict with democratic principles. In France, for example, the view that riots and other large-scale internal disturbances should not be repressed violently by military force but rather managed in a more "civilized" manner by specialized police units gave rise to the creation of the Mobile Gendarmerie (Gendarmerie mobile) in the early 1920s, which subsequently became the main force responsible for dealing with large-scale demonstrations and similar public order challenges.[26]

Gendarmeries in peace operations

Finally, gendarmeries have risen in prominence in international peace operations, another key area of the post-Cold War security agenda. Since the early 1990s there has not only been a massive increase in the number of multilateral peacekeeping missions, but these have also changed fundamentally in nature. While the peacekeeping operations of the Cold War period were typically limited to the deployment of an interposition force between warring factions, the missions that have taken place from the early 1990s onwards have become much more complex, comprising not only military but also a number of civilian, humanitarian and internal security or public order tasks in the target countries. While police forces have generally come to play a much more important role in peace operations, and have been deployed in ever-larger numbers in such missions, it is gendarmerie-type forces in particular that have come to prominence. Precisely because such agencies combine the skills, characteristics and equipment of police and military forces, and because they may be deployed under both civilian and military command, gendarmerie-type forces are often ideally suited for addressing the internal security and public order challenges common in post-war reconstruction efforts. The fact that most gendarmerie personnel have at least some military training, and use heavier equipment than ordinary police forces, makes them ideally suited for operating in destabilized or "non-benign" environments characteristic of countries emerging from war. Moreover, given their military status, gendarmeries are usually easier and faster to deploy in an international operation than would be the case for civilian police forces.[27]

Evidence of the growing importance of gendarmeries in this respect can be seen, for example, in the creation and institutionalization of multinational specialized units (MSUs), which are peace support units composed exclusively of police forces with military status. Such units were set up for the first time in Bosnia in 1998 to take over law enforcement and public order tasks from NATO contingents, and since then MSUs have become a common instrument in peace operations. Subsequently, in 2005 five EU member states (France, Italy, the Netherlands, Portugal and Spain) launched the European Gendarmerie Force (EUROGENDFOR) as a special police rapid reaction force composed solely of police with military status.[28] EUROGENDFOR is based in Vicenza, Italy, and has a core staff of around 900 personnel, with an additional 2,300 available on standby. In 2007 EUROGENDFOR participated in its first EU crisis management project, Operation ALTHEA in Bosnia-Herzegovina. Subsequently, EUROGENDFOR also took part in the NATO-led International Security Assistance Force (ISAF) mission in Afghanistan, as well as the UN Mission in Haiti (MINUSTAH), launched after the country was devastated by an earthquake in 2010.

***

Overall, there is thus considerable evidence of the growing importance of gendarmerie forces in the contemporary European security landscape. Not only have these agencies witnessed a significant expansion – arguably growing more than all other major security forces in Europe – but they have also played a key role in addressing many of the most important security challenges, ranging from border control and counterterrorism to ensuring public order and working in international peace operations.

This section has documented the rise of gendarmerie forces in Western European countries over recent decades in the sense of both an expansion of these forces and their increasingly prominent role in addressing major security challenges. The following sections will look at institutional developments within European gendarmerie forces, which at least to some extent seem to point towards an opposite trend: the increasing demilitarization or "civilianization" of gendarmeries.

DEMILITARIZING THE GENDARMERIE? THE CASES OF FRANCE, ITALY AND SPAIN

The demilitarization, or civilianization, of gendarmerie forces relates to a reduction of their military characteristics and their transformation into more civilian-style police. While an in-depth analysis of such a trend would need to cover a range of dimensions, including changes in military culture or discipline, the main focus here is on institutional transformations, which at least potentially also touch upon the key feature of gendarmeries, namely their formal military status. This trend of (institutional) demilitarization or civilianization is examined by focusing on the largest gendarmerie-type forces in Western Europe: the French Gendarmerie, the Italian Carabinieri and the Spanish Guardia Civil.

The French Gendarmerie

The French National Gendarmerie has been, as already mentioned, the model for most existing gendarmerie-type forces. While its main mission has always been to ensure law and order on the national territory, since its inception it has also been formally part of the armed forces, and its officers have the official status of soldiers. In organizational terms, the French Gendarmerie was controlled mainly by the Defence Ministry until 2002, although especially at the level of the *régions* and *départements* the Interior Ministry (via the prefect) has also held responsibility over the Gendarmerie. Despite its attachment to the Defence Ministry, the director-general of the

French National Gendarmerie (2012)	
Founded:	1791
Personnel:	98,155
Annual budget:	€7.7 billion
Principal ministry:	Before 2004: Defence
	Since 2009: Interior
Part of armed forces:	Yes
Military equipment/training:	Some
Director-General:	Civilian/military
Right to join unions:	No
Regulated working hours:	No
Personnel in international peace operations:	Approx. 350
Number of operations:	12

Gendarmerie may be either a civilian or a military officer, although since 2004 all directors-general have come from the military.

Pursuant to its military status, the French Gendarmerie is structured along military lines and uses a military ranking system. It also has some military-style armoury, in addition to police equipment, such as armoured vehicles, helicopters, light infantry weapons and boats. The initial training of gendarmerie personnel is essentially military in nature and for a small number of recruits is conducted jointly with other members of the French armed forces, although non-commissioned officers (NCOs) of the Gendarmerie are trained in separate dedicated facilities. While the main functions of the Gendarmerie are in policing and law enforcement, it also has a subsidiary military role in defence, although this now represents only around 5 per cent of its operational activities. In the event of war, the Gendarmerie would both act as military police and also perform several more directly combat-related roles, such as protecting certain sensitive sites, gathering intelligence and ensuring territorial coverage.[29]

The military status of the French Gendarmerie has several other implications for the role and character of the force. First, given that gendarmerie personnel are formally considered soldiers, they do not have the right to strike or join unions. Second, the personnel are obliged, at least in principle, to be "permanently available". In contrast to civilian police officers, there is no legal limit on their working hours, and gendarmerie personnel have no claim to compensation for overtime, for example. In further contrast to civilian police, gendarmes are housed in accommodation provided by the state, which is sometimes military barracks.

Within the French police system there has traditionally been a territorial division of labour, in that the Gendarmerie has been responsible for maintaining law and order in rural areas, and the country's civilian national-level police force, the National Police (Police Nationale) for policing the cities. Under this division, the Gendarmerie has covered around 95 per cent of the national territory and around 50 per cent of the population. In their respective areas of responsibility, both police forces have performed the whole spectrum of law enforcement functions, ranging from judicial to administrative policing and public order tasks.

As discussed previously, the Gendarmerie has arguably been the fastest-expanding security force in France over the last three decades – at least as compared to the regular armed forces and the National Police. Moreover, the French Gendarmerie has played an increasingly prominent role in addressing many current security challenges, ranging from counterterrorism to international peace operations.[30] At the same time, however, the evolution of the French Gendarmerie in recent years has also been characterized by its increasing demilitarization or "civilianization" in two main respects: authority over the Gendarmerie has been gradually, although not completely, transferred from the Defence Ministry to the Interior Ministry, and efforts have been made to strengthen cooperation and convergence between the Gendarmerie and the National Police.

The first steps in this direction were taken with a major reform of the French internal security system initiated in 2002. A decree passed in May 2002 transferred authority over the Gendarmerie's internal security missions to the Interior Ministry, while the Defence Ministry remained responsible for the Gendarmerie's military missions, as well as personnel issues and budget.[31] In line with this transfer of responsibility, the role of the prefect (as a subordinate of the Interior Ministry) has also been strengthened, in that he/she has been given an overarching coordination role in internal security matters at the level of the *départements*.[32] Moreover, to strengthen cooperation between the Gendarmerie and the National Police, regional intervention brigades (*groupes d'intervention régionaux*) were created to bring together officers of both forces, as well as members of other institutions, such as customs and fiscal authorities. The main mission of the brigades is to combat violent crime, illegal trafficking and the illegal economy, especially in certain designated "sensitive areas".[33] There are currently around 30 such joint brigades, composed of some 400 officers, of whom around two-thirds are under the command of the National Police with the remainder under the Gendarmerie.[34]

A more far-reaching reform of the country's internal security system was launched in 2009, and has been considered by some as historic. This reform involved a further strengthening of the powers of the Interior Ministry over the Gendarmerie, by placing practically all aspects of its control and function within the remit of this ministry, including its budget, although not military missions or disciplinary matters. Moreover, the authority of the prefect over the Gendarmerie has been further strengthened in that the formal procedure (so-called *réquisition*) which the prefect had to follow to deploy Gendarmerie units has been abolished. However, even though the Gendarmerie is now controlled mainly by the Interior Ministry, these reforms did not remove its formal military status. Indeed, the new law on the Gendarmerie adopted in 2009 in its first article confirms its status as an "armed force" (*force armée*).[35] As one of the consequences, the prohibition on strike action and forming unions remains in place.

In addition to transferring responsibility for the Gendarmerie to the Interior Ministry, there has been a further rapprochement between the Gendarmerie and the National Police. In 2011 a so-called statutory bridge (*passerelle statutaire*) between the two forces was introduced. Under this arrangement, gendarmes and certain police officers may request a temporary transfer to the other force while remaining at the equivalent hierarchical level. In the first year after its introduction, some 40 officers from both bodies requested such a transfer.

The main rationale behind all these changes has been the creation of greater synergies and coherence within France's internal security system. Duplication between the activities of the Gendarmerie and the National Police should be avoided in the interest of more effective crime prevention and greater efficiency. However, while the civilian characteristics of the Gendarmerie and its collaboration with the National Police have been strengthened, there remains a general consensus that the formal military status of the Gendarmerie should be maintained. Having a police force with a military status is seen not only as a key element of France's dual police system, but the Gendarmerie's typical characteristics such as its permanent availability and its strict sense of discipline are viewed as important assets which would be lost if it were to be fully demilitarized.[36]

The acceptance of the Gendarmerie's military status was also manifest in the adoption of the "Charter of the Gendarme" (*Charte du Gendarme*) shortly after the 2009 reforms. This charter was drafted by representatives of the Gendarmerie itself, as well as several political institutions, such as the French parliament and the Interior Ministry. While it does not have the status of a law, it sets out the basic values and principles that should guide the Gendarmerie in its activities. The initial articles of the charter are devoted mainly to the military status of the Gendarmerie: Article 1 stipulates that the Gendarmerie is an "armed force", and that its members are "fully part of the military community"; Article 2 states that the gendarme "adheres, without reservation, to the general status of soldiers".[37]

Overall, there has thus been a clear trend towards the demilitarization or civilianization of the French Gendarmerie, in the sense that control over the Gendarmerie has been transferred to a great extent to the Interior Ministry, and a number of measures have been taken to enhance collaboration and convergence between the Gendarmerie and the National Police. At the same time, however, the formal military status of the Gendarmerie has been maintained and still seems to go unchallenged, both within and outside the force. While these reforms might be seen as steps towards an eventual merger of the Gendarmerie and the civilian police, this would ultimately require a removal of the Gendarmerie's military status. Moreover, the experiences of other countries that have fully demilitarized their gendarmeries suggest that once a gendarmerie's military status has been revoked, unification with the civilian police is likely to follow (see the following section).

The Italian Carabinieri

The Italian Carabinieri is numerically the largest gendarmerie force in Europe, counting well over 100,000 personnel. The Carabinieri shares many similarities with the French Gendarmerie, although there are also significant differences. As with its French counterpart, the Carabinieri is a hybrid organization, somewhere between a police and a military force. Even though most of its activities are in the area of policing and law enforcement, the Carabinieri is also an integral part of the Italian armed forces. Indeed, the Carabinieri was formally part of the Italian army until 2000, when it was separated and became an armed force (*forza armata*) in its own right, and

Italian Carabinieri (2012)	
Founded:	1814
Personnel:	118,716
Annual budget:	€5.8 billion
Principal ministry:	Defence
Part of armed forces:	Yes
Military equipment/training:	Yes
Commander:	Military
Right to join unions:	No
Regulated working hours:	Yes
Personnel in international peace operations:	Approx. 3,500
Number of operations:	21

the fourth branch of the Italian armed forces after the army, the navy and the air force. As such, it has been involved in all of the country's military conflicts. Similar to the French Gendarmerie (until 2002), the Carabinieri is mainly under the control of the Defence Ministry, although depending on the area concerned, it also reports to the Interior Ministry and other ministries as well.

In some respects, the Carabinieri's military characteristics have been even more pronounced than those of the French Gendarmerie. While the director-general of the French Gendarmerie may be either a civilian or a military officer, the commander of the Carabinieri has always been a general of the army (until 2004) or of the Carabinieri itself (since 2004). In addition, the Carabinieri uses heavier equipment than the French Gendarmerie, including light tanks, aircraft and machine guns, for example. The Carabinieri has also been considerably more active in international peace operations than its French counterpart: so far the Carabinieri has participated in a total of 21 such operations, compared to 12 for the Gendarmerie. Moreover, in recent years some 3,500 carabinieri have been deployed in international operations at any one point in time, which is around ten times more than the French Gendarmerie.

In certain other respects, however, the military status of the Italian Carabinieri has had less far-reaching implications than that of its French counterpart. Even though carabinieri are also prohibited from joining unions and striking, their working hours are regulated in the same way as those of the country's civilian police forces, with the maximum number of working hours per week currently set at 36. The militaristic principle of "permanent availability" of personnel does thus not apply to the Italian Carabinieri in the same way as to the French Gendarmerie. Moreover, only some carabinieri are housed by the state: while lower-ranking Italian Carabinieri officers lodge in military barracks, higher-ranking officers may either chose their own residence or be provided with civilian accommodation by the state.

The status of the Carabinieri within the Italian internal security system is also somewhat different from that of the French Gendarmerie. Rather than only two, Italy has a total of five police forces at the national level: the Carabinieri, the State Police (Polizia di Stato), the Finance Guard (Guardia di Finanza), the State Forestry Corps (Corpo forestale dello Stato) and the Penitentiary Police (Polizia Penitenziaria). Of these, only the Carabinieri and the State Police have a general remit covering all aspects of law enforcement. In principle there is a division of labour between these two forces comparable to the system in France, in that the Carabinieri operates in rural areas and the State Police in the cities, yet in practice this division has not been clearly followed. In contrast to the French case, the Carabinieri is also very much present in the cities, where its activities often overlap with those of the State Police. As a result, around 45 per cent of the country's territory is covered by both police forces, while in the remaining 55 per cent only the Carabinieri is active.[38]

Whereas in recent years the French Gendarmerie has undergone a process of demilitarization, whereby responsibility for the force has in most respects been transferred from the Defence to the Interior Ministry, and several measures have been introduced to strengthen collaboration between the Gendarmerie and the police, in the case of the Carabinieri no such transformations have taken place yet. Although similar changes have been intensely debated, so far few such measures have been implemented. Calls for demilitarizing the Carabinieri and merging it with the State Police have traditionally come primarily from the political left, which has regularly decried the militarization of the Italian police system and the high number of police forces in the country.

While these demands long fell on deaf ears, it is noteworthy that they were at least partly taken up by the right-wing Berlusconi government following the reforms of the French Gendarmerie discussed above. Thus in late 2009 the then interior minister announced plans to consider the transfer of the Carabinieri from the Defence to the Interior Ministry. As in the case of France, the main rationale for this initiative was the strengthening of coherence, efficiency and effectiveness within the country's internal security system. Details of these plans have, however, not been made public, including for example the extent to which the military status of the

Carabinieri would be affected by these reforms.[39] Moreover, even though the timeframe for the reforms was set at two years, to date they have not yet been implemented and the Carabinieri itself has expressed firm opposition to the transfer of authority from the Defence to the Interior Ministry.[40]

Notably, however, the Carabinieri has more recently itself called for a certain modification in its military status, at least as far as working conditions are concerned. In early March 2012 representatives of the Carabinieri declared their dissatisfaction with the fact that they were being treated as "second-class citizens", and demanded that their social security and pension benefits be brought in line with those of civilian public employees in Italy.[41]

Thus while the structural similarities between the French Gendarmerie and Carabinieri remain, the extent of reforms in each case has differed significantly. Thus far, there have been no significant institutional reforms of the Carabinieri, and when it comes to enhancing cooperation between the Carabinieri and the State Police, there have been much less far-reaching changes in Italy compared to France. Even though administrative structures within the Interior Ministry, and in particular the Department of Public Security (Dipartimento della pubblica sicurezza), have been set up to strengthen cooperation between the country's police forces, it is commonly agreed that the lack of coordination remains one of the main weaknesses of the Italian internal security system. In contrast to the French case, there are also no joint units of the Carabinieri and the State Police, and there is no possibility for officers to switch between the two forces.

The Spanish Guardia Civil

The Spanish Guardia Civil is the third major gendarmerie-type force in Europe. It was also modelled on, and bears many similarities to, the French Gendarmerie. Similar to its French and Italian counterparts, the Guardia Civil played a crucial role in Spain's nation-building process in the nineteenth century and the consolidation of central power over the more peripheral areas of the national territory. However, during the Franco era the image of the Guardia Civil suffered considerably, as it was commonly seen as the primary instrument of the regime's effort to crush dissent and opposition.

Compared to the French Gendarmerie and the Italian Carabinieri, the Guardia Civil has since the end of the Franco regime been somewhat closer

<table>
<tr><td colspan="2">The Spanish Guardia Civil (2012)</td></tr>
<tr><td>Founded:</td><td>1844</td></tr>
<tr><td>Personnel:</td><td>84,400</td></tr>
<tr><td>Annual budget:</td><td>€2.7 billion</td></tr>
<tr><td>Principal ministry:</td><td>Interior</td></tr>
<tr><td>Part of armed forces:</td><td>No</td></tr>
<tr><td>Military equipment/training:</td><td>Limited</td></tr>
<tr><td>Director-General:</td><td>Civilian/military</td></tr>
<tr><td>Right to join unions:</td><td>No</td></tr>
<tr><td>Regulated working hours</td><td>Yes</td></tr>
<tr><td>Personnel in international
peace operations:</td><td>Approx. 120</td></tr>
<tr><td>Number of operations:</td><td>18</td></tr>
</table>

to a civilian police force. Thus, in contrast to the former two forces, the Guardia Civil has not been formally part of the Spanish armed forces since the 1970s. Even though the Organic Law on Security Forces (Ley Orgánica 2/1986 de Fuerzas y Cuerpos de Seguridad) stipulates that the Guardia Civil is an "armed institution of military nature" (Article 9), the Spanish Constitution of 1978 does not mention it as part of the country's armed forces (Article 8). Moreover, while the Guardia Civil has a dual dependency between the Defence and Interior Ministries, the role of the Interior Ministry has traditionally been stronger, with the remit of the Defence Ministry basically limited to recruitment, careers and disciplinary questions. Also, the director-general of the Guardia Civil has almost always been a civilian, although in principle the post could be held by a military officer.[42] And the military character of the Guardia Civil is less pronounced in the sense that it has only a limited amount of military-style equipment (mainly light infantry weapons), although in the context of its border control operations in particular it has in recent years used heavier equipment, such as helicopters and oceangoing patrol ships. Finally, only some Guardia Civil officers receive military training. Nevertheless, the Guardia Civil has a subsidiary military defence role comparable to that of its French and Italian counterparts. Thus in the event of war it would automatically come under the control of the Ministry of Defence and participate in defending the country against an external attack.

As for the Guardia Civil's participation in international peace operations, this has been more limited than that of the French Gendarmerie and the Italian Carabinieri, although this is partly due to its smaller size. Thus while the Guardia Civil has taken part in a total of 18 international operation to date – which is in fact more than the French Gendarmerie – the number of guardsmen deployed on average has been limited to around 120 officers.

In terms of human resources, the implications of the Guardia Civil's military status are roughly similar to those for the Italian Carabinieri. Like their French and Italian counterparts, Guardia Civil officers are prohibited from joining unions and going on strike, but, in contrast to French Gendarmerie personnel, their working hours are regulated and currently limited to 37.5 hours per week.

The Guardia Civil's status within the Spanish internal security system is also comparable to the French case, in that it operates mainly in rural areas while responsibility for policing the cities falls to the country's other national police force, the National Police (Policia nacional). In their respective areas of operation, both forces cover all aspects of policing and law enforcement, although in certain specific issues they hold exclusive responsibility. Thus, for example, while the Guardia Civil deals exclusively with issues such as weapons and explosives control, traffic control and monitoring of sea and land borders, the National Police is charged with issuing identity documents, control of border checkpoints and inspection of gambling facilities.[43] Moreover, the Guardia Civil has traditionally played the lead role in the fight against ETA and other forms of terrorism, although this element of the division of labour is not explicitly stipulated by law.

Despite the fact that the Guardia Civil is already more "civilianized" than its French and Italian counterparts, intense debate has emerged in recent years in Spain about its further demilitarization. Demands to this effect have traditionally come mainly from the Spanish socialists, but notably also from within the Guardia Civil itself. In particular, when in opposition the socialist party has called for the demilitarization of the Guardia Civil, although when in government it has so far refrained from implementing any far-reaching reforms. For example, the 2004 electoral programme of the socialist party included a number of proposals aimed at reducing the military character of the Guardia Civil, such as its complete transfer to the Interior Ministry, non-application of the military penal code, introducing the right to join unions and strengthening of cooperation between the Guardia Civil and the National Police.[44]

Similar demands have come from within the Guardia Civil, and more specifically from the United Association of Civil Guards (Asociacion Unificada de Guardia Civiles – AUGC), which is the largest organization of Guardia Civil personnel, counting some 25,000 members or approximately a third of the force.[45] Following the electoral victory of the Spanish socialist party in 2005, the AUGC put forward 20 proposals for the "modernization" of the Guardia Civil, many of which in fact focus on its demilitarization. These proposals included the transfer of the Guardia Civil to the exclusive control of the Interior Ministry, the nomination of a civilian director-general, the non-application of military regulations, including the military penal code, an end to military training, the right to join unions and equal working conditions to those of the civilian police.[46]

More recently, in the context of Spain's severe financial and economic crisis, the AUGC and the largest police union (Sindicato Unificado de Policia) have even called for a merger of the Guardia Civil and the National Police, arguing that this would lead to greater efficiency of police work and result in savings of 30–40 per cent.[47] So far, however, neither the socialist government nor the centre-right government, which came to power in 2012, has implemented any of these reforms. The only significant change, which was introduced by the socialist government in 2008, was to merge the previously separate general directorates of the Guardia Civil and the National Police into one General Directorate of the Police and the Guardia Civil (Dirección General de la Policía y de la Guardia Civil), in an effort to strengthen cooperation between the two bodies.

Thus, as in France and Italy, some quarters have called for the demilitarization of the Guardia Civil and even its merger with the National Police, although so far change has remained limited. The most notable difference to the cases of France and Italy, however, is that within the Guardia Civil itself there is a significant faction, possibly even a majority, which has advocated its complete demilitarization. While representatives of the French Gendarmerie and the Italian Carabinieri have voiced certain demands which would relativize their military status, in particular with regard to aligning their working conditions with those of civilian police, the military status itself appears to remain unchallenged within these forces.

***

Even though Europe's three main gendarmerie forces share many similarities in terms of both their formal military status and their functions, there are also some significant differences between them, including with regard to their military characteristics. It can be argued that the Italian Carabinieri remains the most militarized of the three in terms of institutional affiliation, weaponry and training. Differences also persist in how demilitarization is viewed within each context, with the Spanish Guardia Civil, for example, adopting a more favourable position. Demilitarization and civilianization may in fact prove to be a crucial element of whether gendarmeries persist in their separate institutional form, as the following discussion of the cases of Austria and Belgium suggests.

DISSOLVING THE GENDARMERIE: THE CASES OF AUSTRIA AND BELGIUM

While the preceding section highlights a trend towards or at least a debate over the (institutional) demilitarization or civilianization of gendarmerie forces in France, Italy and Spain, even more far-reaching developments in this direction have taken place in Austria and Belgium, leading in these cases to the dissolution of the gendarmerie. Both countries used to have a gendarmerie, which at least at one point met the narrow definition of the term in that they were police forces with formal military status. In both countries, however, the gendarmerie was dissolved and merged with the civilian police. This section traces developments in these two countries.

The Austrian Federal Gendarmerie

When it was created in the early nineteenth century, the Austrian Federal Gendarmerie (Bundesgendarmerie) was modelled largely on the French Gendarmerie. As in the French version, it was originally controlled mainly by the Defence Ministry and formally part of the armed forces (of the Austro-Hungarian Empire).[48] In contrast to many of its European counterparts, however, the Austrian Gendarmerie was brought under exclusive control of the Interior Ministry in the late nineteenth century, which implied that it lost its military status and its formal ties to the regular military were severed.[49] Thus in practically all respects the Federal Gendarmerie was demilitarized much earlier than in other European cases, with the vestiges of its military origins visible only in its military organizational structure and its use of at least some military-style light infantry weapons.

Within the Austrian internal security system, again following the French model, the Gendarmerie was responsible for rural areas, where it carried out practically all law enforcement tasks, while the country's other national police force, the Federal Police (Bundespolizei), operated in larger cities. The Federal Gendarmerie thus provided security for around two-thirds of the population, covering approximately 98 per cent of the Austrian national territory.

Comparable to other European countries, the Federal Gendarmerie underwent considerable expansion from the early 1990s. Between 1990 and 2000, as shown in Table 1, it grew from about 11,000 to around 15,000 officers. As in many other EU countries, the main driving force behind this expansion was the growing concern with irregular immigration, especially across the country's eastern borders following the dissolution of the former Soviet bloc. In the early 1990s a specialized border guard unit, the Border Gendarmerie (Grenzgendarmerie) was created within the Federal Gendarmerie. Its main task was to prevent undocumented migration, human smuggling and other forms of cross-border criminality. By the end of the 1990s this unit comprised around 3,000 officers, accounting for around a fifth of the Gendarmerie's total force.[50]

However, while the Austrian Federal Gendarmerie grew rapidly from 1990 onwards, in 2005 it was disbanded and merged with the Federal Police. This occurred in the context of a major reform of the country's internal security system, initiated in 2002. There had been efforts to increase synergies between the Gendarmerie and the Federal Police, in particular in the areas of logistics and equipment, prior to the merger, yet the dissolution of the Gendarmerie came as a surprise. As late as 2000 the then minister of the interior, Ernst Strasser, had denied the existence of plans to merge the two bodies, arguing that a unification of the Gendarmerie and the Federal Police would be comparable to the "Dalai Lama demanding a merger of the Catholic and Protestant Churches".[51]

Yet in 2002 the aforementioned reform of the internal security system was launched, widely agreed to be the most far-reaching administrative reform initiative in Austria in the post-Second World War period. Its main objectives were to strengthen the effectiveness of the country's police in the fight against crime. As a part of this initiative, the merger of the two forces was intended to simplify the country's police system and prevent duplications. Administrative structures were to become leaner, while the police would have a stronger presence on the streets. At least officially, the main goal was to enhance the effectiveness of police action, while cost savings were seen as less immediately relevant.[52]

Even though the police reform project and the merger of the Gendarmerie with the Federal Police were generally seen as a success, some objections were raised. Criticism has come in particular from former members of the police, who argued that the reforms have led to overcentralization of the country's internal system and a "gendarmization" of the police, in that the police have come to be dominated by an overly strict sense of discipline and the principle of "blind obedience" to superiors.[53]

The Belgian Gendarmerie

Similar developments have taken place in Belgium, where the Gendarmerie has also been disbanded and merged with the country's civilian police. The Belgian Gendarmerie (Rijkswacht/Gendarmerie nationale) was yet another carbon copy of the French Gendarmerie. Like its French counterpart, it was a police force with a formal military status, organized along military lines and controlled mainly by the Defence Ministry. Comparable to the French Gendarmerie and the Italian Carabinieri, it was considered an integral part of the country's armed forces (its fourth branch alongside the army, navy and air force). The principal difference to the French internal security system was that Belgium traditionally had three rather than two police forces: the Gendarmerie, which operated at the national (federal) level; the municipal police, which was responsible for law enforcement at the level of the municipalities; and the judicial police, which dealt with criminal investigations.

However, in the 1990s the Belgium Gendarmerie underwent a process of (institutional) demilitarization, which ultimately led to its dissolution. The origins of this change go back to the 1980s, when Belgium was experiencing a growing threat from internal terrorism and rising criminality, and the country's law enforcement agencies were commonly seen as ineffective in responding to these challenges. The Easter Agreements (Accords de la Pentecôte) were adopted by the governing parties to remedy these deficiencies; their main objective was to improve cooperation between, and thus the effectiveness of, the country's three police forces.[54] As far as the Gendarmerie was concerned, the agreements removed its military status and brought it under the sole responsibility of the Interior Ministry.[55]

Only a few years later, however, a much more far-reaching reform of the Belgian internal security system was launched, under which the Gendarmerie was dissolved entirely. Experts had already slated the creation of a unified police system in Belgium during the negotiation of the Easter Agreements, but it was only in response to the so-called Dutroux affair that more general consensus around this relatively radical measure emerged. The Dutroux affair was the case of a serial killer and child molester who had kidnapped, abused and killed several children during the 1980s and 1990s. The fact that Dutroux was able to commit these crimes over many years and go undetected was attributed to the lack of cooperation and unhealthy rivalries between the country's police forces.[56] A new system based on an integrated police was thus created, whereby the Gendarmerie was merged with the former judicial police into a new, and entirely civilian, Federal Police, while the municipal police was transformed into 196 local police forces. While the local units are responsible for basic law enforcement tasks within their respective jurisdictions, the Federal Police deals with specialized police tasks, as well as issues affecting several local jurisdictions. Instead of a hierarchical relationship between the two levels, a relationship based on a functional division of labour between local- and federal-level police forces has been established.

***

The cases of Austria and Belgium demonstrate that once consensus on the military character of gendarmerie forces is broken, a move to dissolve and merge these forces with civilian police can easily follow. While the specific conditions leading to this change in status were different in each case, and the timelines for these reforms also varied widely, both cases reflect a similar progression in this regard. They also show that while the dissolution of the gendarmerie and its merger with the civilian police might lead to stronger centralization of the internal security system, this need not necessarily be the case. In Austria there have indeed been at least some concerns that the unification of the Gendarmerie with the police and the move away from the dual police system has led to an overcentralization of the country's police. In the case of Belgium, by contrast, the new system of an integrated police, at least in principle, seems more decentralized than the country's previous police system.

Having discussed the role and transformation of gendarmerie-type forces in the European context, the focus now turns to countries of the Middle East and North Africa, where such hybrid security agencies are also quite common. The purpose of this comparison is to examine whether similar trends as those identified in the preceding sections can also be observed beyond the European context.

LOOKING SOUTH: GENDARMERIES IN THE MAGHREB AND TURKEY

Gendarmerie-type forces are not only important elements of the coercive apparatus of European countries, but also – or even more so – in countries of the developing world. Hybrid security agencies combining police and military characteristics can be found in many countries in Africa, the Middle East and Latin America. The importance of such intermediary security forces in less developed states was first documented by Morris Janowitz. Writing in 1977, he noted that the growth of the security apparatus of many developing countries since the 1960s had involved, first and foremost, an expansion of paramilitary or gendarmerie-type forces, whose growth rates often exceeded those of the regular military.[57] Janowitz viewed such forces primarily as instruments used by authoritarian regimes – both military and civilian – to maintain themselves in power. He argued that while in many developing countries the regular military played an important internal role, in the long run the armed forces would be reluctant to become too deeply involved in the "distasteful task of internal security", which would put a strain on its coherence and legitimacy. As a result, the military would tend to rely on paramilitary or gendarmerie-type forces for control of the civilian population.[58]

More recently, the growth of gendarmerie-type forces in less developed countries has been analysed by Sunil Dasgupta, who provides a somewhat different explanation of this development. He argues that the spread of democratic norms and human rights has meant that leaders of developing countries have become increasingly reluctant to resort to the use

     Derek Lutterbeck

Table 2: Evolution of manpower of regular military and gendarmerie-type forces in Algeria, Morocco, Tunisia and Turkey, 1980–2010

		1980	1990	2000	2010
Algeria	Armed forces	101,000	125,500	124,000	147,000
	Gendarmerie	10,000	23,000	60,000	130,000
Morocco	Armed forces	116,500	192,500	198,500	195,800
	Gendarmerie	n.a.	10,000	12,000	20,000
Tunisia	Armed forces	28,600	38,000	35,000	35,800
	National Guard	1,000	10,000	12,000	12,000
Turkey	Armed forces	567,000	647,400	609,700	510,600
	Gendarmerie	120,000	70,000	218,000	205,000

Source: International Institute for Strategic Studies, *Military Balance* (London: IISS, 1981, 1991, 2001 and 2011). For the Algerian Gendarmerie, *Military Balance* gives the figure of 20,000 for 2010, which stands in sharp contrast to local sources, according to which the Gendarmerie counts some 130,000 men (see endnote 61). The same applies to the manpower of the Turkish Gendarmerie in 2010, which also seems to be vastly underreported in *Military Balance* (see endnote 82).

of regular armed forces to suppress internal dissent, relying instead on gendarmerie-type or constabulary forces for the maintenance of public order.[59] Thus while both authors highlighted a trend towards military retreat from internal security missions and the replacement of regular armed forces by gendarmerie-type or other hybrid agencies in this area, they have attributed these developments to somewhat different factors: the military's inherent reluctance to become involved in domestic security missions, on the one hand, and external pressures arising from the global spread of human rights norms on the other.

The aim of this section is to build on the previous analysis of gendarmerie forces in Europe by examining their evolution in another regional context: the Middle East and North Africa. The analysis focuses on three former French colonies, Algeria, Morocco and Tunisia, all of which have followed the French dual police model. This should allow for a meaningful comparison with European gendarmeries. Moreover, the case of Turkey will also be taken into account, which too has adopted the French model (as a result of more indirect influence[60]), and whose gendarmerie is the largest in the region, possibly even globally.

Table 2 depicts the evolution of the manpower of regular military and gendarmerie-type forces in the four countries from 1980 to 2010. While both militaries and gendarmeries have expanded over this period, the growth rates of gendarmerie forces have been significantly higher, amounting to around 60 per cent compared to less than 10 per cent for the armed forces. In this context as well, gendarmerie-type forces thus seem to have gained in importance relative to the regular military.

Even though the gendarmeries of the four countries analysed here share a number of commonalities, there are also some significant differences in terms of both functions and characteristics. As argued in the following, these divergences can be explained with regard to differences in the political regimes of the four countries, as well as the security challenges they have confronted.

The Algerian Gendarmerie

The Algerian Gendarmerie (2012)	
Founded:	1962
Personnel:	130,000
Annual budget:	n.a.
Principal ministry:	Defence
Part of armed forces:	Yes
Military equipment/training:	Yes
Commander:	Military
Right to join unions:	No
Regulated working hours:	No

By far the largest gendarmerie force of the three Maghreb countries, in both absolute and relative terms, is the Algerian National Gendarmerie (Gendarmerie nationale). Although there are conflicting reports on its size (and no published official data), the most credible information suggests that the Algerian Gendarmerie currently counts some 130,000 men – which is also far larger than any comparable force in Europe.[61] At the time of independence in 1962 the Algerian Gendarmerie reportedly had only around 3,000 officers, meaning it has grown more than 40-fold since then.

Given the lack of detailed information about its size and character, it is difficult to say what has driven this massive expansion of the Algerian Gendarmerie, but it is reasonable to assume that an important factor was the "civil war" (the expression itself is contested) of the 1990s, during which the Algerian regime was embroiled in a bloody struggle with an Islamist insurgency that lasted for almost ten years and left up to 200,000 dead.[62] Indeed, in the initial phases of the conflict it was the Gendarmerie that stood at the forefront of the battle with the Islamists, because it was the only security force in the country that was trained and equipped for counterinsurgency operations, whereas the armed forces were insufficiently prepared to deal with such domestic challenges.[63] While the Gendarmerie ultimately proved unable to master the situation alone, and the military subsequently took control of the country's counterterrorism operations, the Gendarmerie continued to play an important part in fighting the rebellion. For example, the special 60,000-strong anti-guerrilla force created in the 1990s, which spearheaded the government's counterinsurgency effort, was composed of both military and Gendarmerie units.[64]

Just like other gendarmerie-type forces, the Algerian Gendarmerie is responsible for maintaining law and order in rural areas, while the country's other national-level police force, the Sûreté Nationale, operates in larger cities. While the Gendarmerie performs practically all law enforcement duties in its field of operations, it also has a number of specialized units. These include notably its elite counterterrorist unit (*détachement spécial d'intervention*), which has played a key role in the country's counterterrorism operations, including during the recent hostage crisis at the In Amenas gas plant.[65]

While the struggle against the Islamist insurgency has arguably been a main driving force behind the expansion of the Gendarmerie, its characteristics have been closely related to the nature of the Algerian regime itself. Since independence, Algeria has been governed by a military-based regime where effective political power has been held by the military leadership. Deriving its legitimacy from its key role in the country's struggle for independence from France, the Algerian military has been the main source of political power. Even though Algeria has maintained a facade of civilian leadership in the form of a civilian presidency and government, the military has controlled practically all important policy areas, ranging from national security to key economic issues. It has also held *de facto* veto power over the presidency, and has on occasion removed presidents from office when their policies were not to its liking.[66]

This predominant role of the military in Algeria has also been reflected in its practically complete control over the Gendarmerie. The latter has been fully integrated into and controlled by the Algerian armed forces. The Algerian Gendarmerie is answerable exclusively to the Defence Ministry, which is practically an extension of the armed forces and headed by a senior military officer. The Gendarmerie itself has always been commanded by a military general. Moreover, in recent years the military has reportedly strengthened its grip over the Gendarmerie, at least in the area of counterterrorism, as the armed forces have assumed overall command of both the Gendarmerie and the police in the fight against terrorist organizations active in the country.[67]

The Algerian Gendarmerie has been heavily militarized not only in institutional terms but also in other respects. It is organized along military lines, uses a military ranking system and has a considerable amount of military-style equipment, such as light infantry weapons, armoured vehicles and helicopters.

Ultimately, two main features of the Algerian Gendarmerie stand out. First, it is a very large force comparatively, which has arguably been a consequence of the severe internal challenges the country has confronted in the form of a large-scale insurgency against the regime. Second, reflecting the military-dominated nature of Algeria's regime, the Gendarmerie has also been firmly integrated into the country's armed forces. Even though the Algerian Gendarmerie is basically a police force, it has been more tightly controlled by the military than any of the other gendarmeries discussed in this paper.

The Moroccan Royal Gendarmerie

The Moroccan Gendarmerie (2012)	
Founded:	1957
Personnel:	22,000
Annual budget:	n.a.
Principal controlling body:	King
Part of armed forces:	Yes
Military equipment/training:	Yes
Commander:	Military
Right to join unions:	No
Regulated working hours:	No

The Moroccan Royal Gendarmerie (Gendarmerie Royale) is only a fraction of the size of its Algerian counterpart. Even though the two countries have a roughly equal population (but Algeria has a much larger territory), the Royal Gendarmerie counts a mere 22,000 men. It can be assumed that the fact that Morocco has not experienced the same kind of internal turmoil as Algeria at least in part explains the Moroccan Gendarmerie's much smaller size. Even though Morocco has been involved in a long-standing struggle over Western

Sahara against the Polisario, this conflict has been largely confined to the contested areas and did not spread throughout Morocco's territory in the same way that Algeria's Islamist insurgency did.

Despite its more limited manpower, however, the Royal Gendarmerie is considered an elite force within the Moroccan armed forces: only the most talented graduates of the country's military academy are recruited into the Gendarmerie. It is also well funded, reportedly absorbing almost a quarter (22 per cent) of the country's military budget, whereas the army takes a mere 17 per cent.[68]

The Moroccan Royal Gendarmerie again follows the French model in being responsible for maintaining law and order in rural areas. As is the case with other gendarmerie-type forces, it too includes several specialized branches, the most renowned of which is its special anti-terrorist unit (*groupe d'intervention gendarmerie royale*). The unit has been upgraded considerably as the Gendarmerie has increasingly come to focus on counterterrorism operations, in particular since the terrorist attacks on Casablanca in May 2003.[69]

Similar to the Algerian Gendarmerie, the Moroccan Royal Gendarmerie is formally part of the country's armed forces. It is structured along military lines, uses a military ranking system and part of the training of gendarmerie personnel is done jointly with the army. The Royal Gendarmerie also has a significant amount of heavy equipment, including light infantry weapons, helicopters and even a few surveillance airplanes.

In other respects, however, the Moroccan Royal Gendarmerie differs considerably from its Algerian counterpart. These differences can be largely explained by the nature of the Moroccan regime. In contrast to Algeria, where the military has been the main pillar of the regime and has *de facto* controlled all major policy areas, Morocco is a hereditary monarchy where ultimate power is vested in the king. This political arrangement is reflected in the fact that one of the main tasks of the Moroccan Royal Gendarmerie has been to ensure the security of the king and his entourage – this gained particular importance after two failed military coups against the Moroccan king in the early 1970s. Since then one of the principal functions of the Royal Gendarmerie has been to monitor the regular military to prevent potential conspiracies against the king. One military analyst has described the Gendarmerie as "the King's eye on the troops".[70]

As a result, the Moroccan Royal Gendarmerie has enjoyed much greater independence from the regular military compared to the Algerian Gendarmerie.[71] Even though the Gendarmerie is, as mentioned, formally integrated into the armed forces, it reports directly to the king and has been commanded by a close confidant of the king (General Hosni Benslimane) for more than 40 years. There is also no real defence ministry in Morocco, as the ministry was disbanded in the aftermath of the aforementioned coup attempts and replaced by a purely administrative structure, with the king exercising overall strategic control over the armed forces.[72] Finally, military control over the Gendarmerie has also been more limited due to the fact that the Moroccan Royal Gendarmerie is answerable to the Interior and Justice Ministries in addition to the defence administration.

The Tunisian National Guard

The Tunisian National Guard (2012)	
Founded:	1957
Personnel:	15,000
Annual budget:	n.a.
Principal ministry:	Interior
Part of armed forces:	No
Military equipment/training:	Yes
Commander:	Civilian/military
Right to join unions:	Yes (since 2011)
Regulated working hours:	No

While the Algerian and Moroccan Gendarmeries are heavily militarized and fully integrated into their national armed forces, the Tunisian equivalent – the National Guard (Garde nationale) – has not followed this pattern. When it was first created in 1957 the National Guard was part of the Tunisian armed forces and controlled by the Defence Ministry, as is typical of gendarmerie forces. However, during the first years of the country's independence the National Guard was transferred entirely to the Interior Ministry, arguably because Tunisia's first leader, Habib Bourguiba, generally distrusted the military and sought to ensure the primacy of civilian over military power.[73] Moreover, for both Bourguiba and even more so his successor, Zine El Abidine Ben Ali, the Interior Ministry and not the armed forces served as the main power base.[74]

Being answerable only to the Interior Ministry and not being part of the armed forces, members of the Tunisian National Guard do not have the formal status of soldiers. The official designation of the National Guard is somewhat ambiguous; the most recent law on the force describes it as a "civilian armed force" (*force armée civile*).[75] In practice, however, the implications of the National Guard's "civilian" status have been limited, as most features typically deriving from a gendarmerie's military status apply to the Tunisian National Guard as well: it is organized along military lines and uses a military-style ranking system. Its members also do military training and are housed in barracks, and it has some military equipment, such as light infantry weapons.[76] Moreover, at least prior to the changes initiated in 2011, National Guardsmen were prohibited from going on strike or joining unions, and their working hours were in practice unregulated (a feature which applied even to the country's civilian police).[77]

Compared to the two other Maghreb countries, Tunisia reflects a relatively unusual situation where the Interior Ministry has held exclusive control over both the gendarmerie and the country's other national-level police, the Sûreté Nationale. Despite this, however, collaboration between these two forces was reportedly very limited, at least under Ben Ali's rule. Indeed, a major concern of the Tunisian autocrat was to keep the two forces separate and in competition, so as to prevent any challenge against his regime arising from within the internal security apparatus. Ben Ali thus generally discouraged cooperation and sought to fuel rivalries between the National Guard and the police.[78]

The Tunisian National Guard has thus traditionally been less militarized than the Algerian and Moroccan Gendarmeries, at least in terms of its institutional affiliation. Moreover, in the context of the recent transformations in the region, which began in Tunisia and then spread to other countries, and are commonly referred to as the "Arab Spring", at least some modest steps towards the demilitarization of the National Guard, as well as the police, have been taken. Such changes have been demanded both from within the internal security forces and by the country's new (interim) leadership. Almost immediately after Ben Ali's downfall, for the first time in the country's history, Tunisian police and National Guardsmen took to the streets demanding better working conditions and the right to join unions, among other things. In March 2011 the interim government lifted the prohibition on members of the security forces joining unions, and shortly thereafter the first unions of police and National Guardsmen were formed.[79] Other items on the country's emerging security sector reform agenda have included better regulation of working hours and the potential merger of the National Guard with the police (although it remains unclear as to what extent the latter measure is supported within these forces themselves).[80] The demilitarization of the country's internal security apparatus has thus become an integral part of Tunisia's nascent democratization agenda, even though reforms in this direction have been limited so far.

The Turkish Gendarmerie

The Turkish Gendarmerie (2012)	
Founded:	1836
Personnel:	205,103
Annual budget:	n.a.
Principal ministry:	Defence
Part of armed forces:	Yes
Military equipment/training:	Yes
Commander:	Military
Right to join unions:	No
Regulated working hours:	No

By far the largest gendarmerie force in absolute terms in the Euro-Mediterranean region (and possibly even globally) is the Turkish Gendarmerie (Jandarma).[81] With more than 200,000 officers, it is even bigger than its Algerian counterpart, although relative to population size the Turkish Gendarmerie is slightly smaller.[82] As in the case of Algeria, the comparatively large size of the Turkish Gendarmerie can arguably be explained by the rather severe internal security challenges the country has faced, in the form of the Kurdish separatist movement and, in particular, the activities of the Kurdistan Workers' Party (PKK). Since the mid-1980s the Turkish government has been involved in a violent struggle against the PKK, which has demanded independence for the Kurdish-inhabited areas as well as better political and cultural rights for Kurds inside Turkey. According to official figures, the conflict between the Turkish regime and the Kurdish separatists, which has been waged in particular in the southeastern parts of the country, has cost some 40,000 lives since the 1980s.

The Turkish Gendarmerie has played a key role in fighting the Kurdish rebellion. While counterinsurgency operations have generally been carried out under the overall command of the Turkish armed forces, the Turkish Gendarmerie, and in particular its anti-terrorism units (the so-called special teams), has been deployed on a regular basis against the PKK.[83] Moreover, the Gendarmerie has also been responsible for creating and managing the village guard system, which has been a core element of the government's effort to combat the Kurdish insurgency.[84]

When it was first created in the mid-nineteenth century by the Ottoman rulers, the Gendarmerie was, like other gendarmerie-type forces, an integral part of the armed forces of the Ottoman Empire. Even though its main task has been to ensure law and order in rural areas, it was also involved in all of the Ottoman Empire's major military conflicts, including the First World War and Turkey's war of independence. Since the creation of the Turkish Republic in 1923, the nature and role of the Turkish Gendarmerie have been a reflection of Turkey's military-dominated regime. Not unlike Algeria, the Turkish military has traditionally formed the backbone of the country's regime, and military coups against elected governments have posed a regular threat, even though military influence has receded considerably over recent years, partly as a result of Turkey's EU accession process. As a consequence of these political dynamics, and comparable to Algeria, the Turkish military has always exercised relatively tight control over the Turkish Gendarmerie. Thus up until the 1980s the Turkish Gendarmerie was under exclusive control of the Defence Ministry, which itself was largely dominated by the armed forces.[85] According to the most recent legislation on the Turkish Gendarmerie (Law No. 2803 of 3 October 1983), which was introduced after the 1980 military coup, the Gendarmerie has a *de jure* dual affiliation: while it remains part of the Turkish armed forces and subject to the general staff for "all duties pertaining to the armed forces", as well as training and education, the Interior Ministry holds responsibility over tasks "related to public security and order" (Article 4). It is, however, commonly agreed among Turkish observers that the armed forces and the general staff have retained real *de facto* power over the Gendarmerie, and that the role of the Interior Ministry and the regional civilian authorities remains very limited at best.[86]

In other aspects as well, the Turkish Gendarmerie is a heavily militarized institution. Up to 80 per cent of its members are recruited through compulsory military service, and education remains dominated by military training, with limited attention given to law enforcement issues, especially as far as NCOs are concerned.[87] The Turkish Gendarmerie has always been commanded by a military general and is organized along military lines. Moreover, it uses even more military-style equipment than most other gendarmerie-type forces, including heavy machine guns, grenade launchers, armoured vehicles and helicopters.

However, in recent years there have been efforts to demilitarize the Turkish Gendarmerie and bring it closer to being a civilian police force. As with other security sector reform efforts in Turkey, an important driving force in this regard has been the EU, which in the context of Turkey's accession process has been pushing for demilitarization and the strengthening of civilian control over the Gendarmerie.[88] One of the EU's key demands in this regard has been to transform the Gendarmerie General Command into a primarily civilian body, comparable to the reforms of the Turkish National Security Council, which also used to be a military-dominated institution but is nowadays dominated by civilians.[89] However, such measures have not been implemented so far, reportedly due to resistance within the Turkish general staff.[90] The most significant reform in recent years has been to abolish the so-called EMASYA protocol, which gave the military the authority to take action in civilian affairs without approval by the civilian authorities.[91] In mid-2013 a new "civilian" protocol was adopted which gives provincial governors the authority to call upon military units in the event of unrest, including the Gendarmerie.[92] At least in principle, the powers of civilian authorities over the Turkish Gendarmerie have thus been strengthened, although it remains to be seen to what extent these new regulations will be implemented.[93]

***

Although all three Maghreb countries and Turkey have adopted the French dual police model with a rural gendarmerie and an urban civilian police, the functions and characteristics of the four gendarmerie forces differ considerably, both among these countries and compared to Western European contexts. The preceding analysis suggests that two main factors can account for these differences: the severity of domestic security challenges, and the nature of the political regime. The more serious the internal security threats the country has been facing, the larger and more important is the role of the gendarmerie. Moreover, the greater the influence of the military within the political system a whole, the more militarized the gendarmerie will be.

CONCLUSIONS

The aim of this paper is to map the evolution of gendarmerie-type forces over the past three decades across the different contexts of Western Europe, the Middle East and North Africa. Describing how gendarmeries across these diverse regions have changed over the past three decades in terms of their functions, institutional characteristics and human and material resources reveals two apparently paradoxical trends. On the one hand, such agencies have generally grown in importance across the regions analysed here, as evidenced by their considerable expansion over recent decades as well as their new roles in addressing many of the most pressing security challenges. Yet on the other hand there has also been a trend towards the demilitarization or civilianization of gendarmeries, especially in some European countries, where this trend has even led to the dissolution of these forces. Before suggesting an explanation of these seemingly contradictory trends, this concluding section compares the main findings of the preceding analysis. It also raises the question of the added value of gendarmeries, and reflects upon the future evolution of such forces.

Comparative insights

The comparative analysis of gendarmeries in Western Europe, the Maghreb countries and Turkey shows that the two overarching trends of expansion and demilitarization can be observed to varying degrees in each case. While in Western European countries a growing concern with transnational (or neither purely internal nor external) security challenges seems to have driven the expansion of gendarmeries, in the Middle Eastern countries analysed here it is those with experiences of large-scale insurgencies that have developed large gendarmerie forces. Furthermore, a link between democratization processes and the demilitarization of internal security (including gendarmeries) is illustrated by the fact that the gendarmerie forces of the Middle East and North Africa are generally more militarized than their European counterparts, reflecting the less democratic nature of these regimes. However, recent steps towards democratization in the region have included efforts – albeit very modest ones – to demilitarize the gendarmerie as well as internal security provision more generally.

In the European context the demilitarization or civilianization of the gendarmerie – at least in institutional terms – has been an issue of debate in all countries studied here. In France, Italy and Spain proposals for reducing the military characteristics of the gendarmeries, bringing them closer to a civilian-style police force, enhancing collaboration between the gendarmeries and the police, or even merging them with the civilian police have been considered by political decision-makers. Yet significant reforms in this direction have so far only been implemented in France, where the Gendarmerie has been brought under almost exclusive control of the Interior Ministry, and fairly far-reaching measures aimed at enhancing cooperation and convergence between the Gendarmerie and the civilian police have been launched. Despite these reforms, however, the military status of the French Gendarmerie has been maintained and, at least so far, seems to retain broad acceptance.

The main rationale behind these reform proposals in all three countries has generally been the streamlining of the internal security system and the promise of greater efficiency and elimination of duplication in police activities. Moreover, the political left has traditionally advanced the argument that internal security and law enforcement should be demilitarized and ultimately entrusted to civilian police forces exclusively. Nevertheless, it is noteworthy that the most significant steps so far taken towards demilitarizing gendarmeries have been made by centre-right governments. For example, the most far-reaching changes of the French Gendarmerie were launched under Sarkozy's centre-right government, while the Berlusconi government in Italy also announced similar plans for the Carabinieri, even though they were not implemented.

A significant difference between the three European countries analysed here is the position of the gendarmeries themselves with regard to the proposed reforms and particular moves towards their demilitarization. In all these countries, representatives of the gendarmeries have called for working conditions on par with their civilian counterparts, which at least to some extent might relativize their military status. Beyond this, however, it is only within the Spanish Guardia Civil that a significant faction, possibly even a majority, has advocated complete demilitarization and even merger with the civilian police.

The path towards dissolution and merger began in a similar way in both Austria and Belgium, where the gendarmeries were disbanded entirely and merged with the civilian police as part of a general reform of the internal security system. Even though the immediate cause was somewhat different in each of the two cases, the overall objective was largely the same as the rationale for demilitarization in other European countries: to improve coordination and cooperation between police forces, and avoid duplication and dysfunctional competition within the internal security system.

In so far as the experiences of these two countries might be relevant for other countries considering reform of their gendarmerie forces, it is suggestive that in both Austria and Belgium the dissolution of the gendarmerie was preceded by the removal of its formal military status. While the Austrian Gendarmerie lost its military status and was transferred to the Interior Ministry as early as the nineteenth century, for the Belgian Gendarmerie this process leading to dissolution unfolded relatively quickly during the 1990s. Austria and Belgium are almost the only European countries that have revoked the formal military status of their gendarmeries,[94] and in both countries this step was ultimately followed by the disbanding of the force and its merger with the civilian police. This suggests that efforts to demilitarize the gendarmeries in other countries are likely to lead to their eventual dissolution and integration into the civilian police, although the Austrian example also highlights that there may be a considerable time lag between the (institutional) demilitarization and dissolution of the gendarmerie.[95]

There are thus considerable differences between individual European countries in terms of how far this process of (institutional) demilitarization of gendarmeries – and of internal security more generally – has moved. Arguably, these divergences are the result of differences in security challenges confronting the countries concerned. It can, for example, be argued that the fact that the Italian Carabinieri is not only the largest but also the most militarized gendarmerie-type force in Europe is a reflection of the seriousness of the internal threats the country faces, particularly from various Mafia organizations. These challenges appear to call for a more "muscular", military-style response, which is probably one reason for the relatively more militarized features of the Carabinieri.

The role of threats to internal security as a driver in the expansion of gendarmerie forces is an insight that carries over to Turkey and the three Maghreb countries analysed in this paper. Hence, of the four countries it is clearly Algeria that has suffered the most severe internal turmoil, with almost a decade of civil war. This fact helps to account for the comparatively large size of the Algerian Gendarmerie. Turkey has also been confronted by considerable domestic challenges in the form of Kurdish separatist movements, which have arguably been an important factor driving the expansion of the Turkish Gendarmerie.

Moreover, the specific features of the political regimes in these four countries have been a decisive factor in influencing the nature of their gendarmeries. Under Algeria's and Turkey's military-dominated regimes, the gendarmeries have been fully integrated into and controlled by the country's military establishment, although recent reform efforts in Turkey have aimed at loosening the military's grip. In Morocco the gendarmerie has also been used as a tool of regime maintenance, but, by contrast, as an instrument of the king rather than the military. As one of the principal functions of the Moroccan Gendarmerie has been to keep a watch on the regular military, it has enjoyed much greater independence from the armed forces than its Algerian or Turkish counterparts. Similarly, Tunisia under Ben Ali can be described as a repressive police state where the Interior Ministry formed the backbone of the regime and the armed forces were kept away from political power. As a consequence, the Tunisian National Guard has been entirely detached from the armed forces and answerable exclusively to the Interior Ministry.

Compared to their European counterparts, the gendarmeries of Turkey and the three Maghreb countries analysed here can generally be described as more heavily militarized forces. The Tunisian National Guard is only partly an exception to this trend: while controlled exclusively by the Interior Ministry and without formal military status, it is comparable to the other gendarmeries of the region in most other respects, ranging from internal organization and training to equipment and working conditions. Again, this suggests that in non- or only partly democratic states, the gendarmeries, as well as internal security forces more generally, tend to be more militarized than in democratic regimes. The recent moves in Tunisia and Turkey towards more democratic rule have raised the issue of the demilitarization of their internal security forces, including the gendarmerie, further highlighting the relationship between democratization processes and the demilitarization of internal security.

Explaining the paradoxical evolution of gendarmeries

The evolution of gendarmerie-type forces in Europe and beyond over the last three decades overall presents a somewhat ambiguous picture. On the one hand, most of these forces have witnessed a considerable expansion and come to assume an increasingly prominent role in addressing many of the most important contemporary security challenges, ranging from border control and counterterrorism to public order tasks and international peace operations. On the other hand, there has been a trend to reduce the military characteristics of these agencies, which in some European countries has gone as far as dissolving the gendarmerie altogether and integrating it into the civilian police. How can these two seemingly contradictory developments be explained? It is argued here that at least two broad – and at least partly opposing – factors or trends can account for the overall evolution of gendarmerie forces.

Starting with the expansion and growing importance of gendarmerie-type forces in recent years, the preceding analysis suggests these have been driven by – and are a manifestation of – the increasing convergence of internal and external security agendas, which in itself has been the result of a number of broad developments, and in particular globalization. It is often argued that developments such as easier travel and advances in communication technologies have given rise to, or increased the significance of, a number of new threats or challenges to security which, in terms of either their spatial dimension or their intensity, are neither purely internal nor purely external in nature. Typically, these include phenomena such as irregular migration, international terrorism and transnational organized crime, all of which are often referred to as the so-called "dark side" of globalization. Such non-conventional security issues may require a more "robust" response than ordinary police forces are usually able to provide, yet not the deployment of the military. It is mainly in addressing such challenges that gendarmerie-type forces have come to play an increasingly prominent role. Given their "hybrid" nature, combining police and military characteristics, gendarmerie-type forces seem ideally suited for dealing with such "hybrid" security issues.

Turning to the "civilianization" or demilitarization of gendarmeries, it can be argued that this seems to be part of a long-term historical trend towards the demilitarization of internal security which has taken place in all liberal-democratic states and can be seen as a key aspect of the democratization process. As has been pointed out by Anthony Giddens and others, one of the main achievements of the liberal-democratic order has been the gradual removal of military forces from the state's domestic sphere and a restriction of their focus to external threats, while responsibility for law and order within the boundaries of the state has come to be assumed by specialized police forces.[96] In most parts of Europe this development was only completed – to various degrees – in the course of the twentieth century, prior to which armed forces were regularly deployed within the borders of the state to quell internal unrest and deal with other serious domestic challenges. The very creation of gendarmeries was, in fact, motivated to a large extent by the aim to reduce the internal role of the military and replace it with forces distinct from the regular military (even if they had a military status).

This is not to say that the demilitarization of internal security has been a linear process without reversals, or that it has proceeded uniformly across European countries. Indeed, it can be argued that in the post-Cold War period in particular this development has been reversed at least to some extent, in so far as the scope of military missions within the borders of the state has increased, a development which has arguably been driven by a number of factors related to the end of the Cold War and the decline in external military threats.[97] Nevertheless, in liberal-democratic states the use of the armed forces for internal security purposes is nowadays commonly seen as an exceptional, rather than an ordinary, measure, and one that is only justified under relatively specific and unusual circumstances.[98] As the use of the armed forces for internal security purposes is often seen as threatening civil liberties and democratic principles, the domestic deployment of military forces is regulated by relatively strict criteria in most democratic regimes. Beyond the European context, the linkage between the demilitarization of internal security and broader democratization processes is also evidenced in recent efforts to demilitarize the gendarmerie (and internal security forces more generally) in countries such as Tunisia and Turkey as they have embarked on a democratization path.

The demilitarization of gendarmeries can thus be seen as a logical continuation of the general process of demilitarization of internal security, which started with the (gradual) removal of regular military forces from the state's domestic realm. Just as the sphere of domestic security has been demilitarized by reducing the internal role of the regular military in favour of police and gendarmerie-type forces, so the demilitarization of gendarmeries represents further movement in this direction.

What added value for gendarmeries?

One key question that any analysis of gendarmeries needs to address concerns their added value in the different areas of security provision with which they are typically concerned. The most commonly advanced argument in favour of gendarmeries is that their hybrid nature and the way they combine police and military characteristics make them particularly suitable for addressing many contemporary challenges. Thus, for example, it is the fact that gendarmeries have heavier equipment and a more centralized structure than civilian police forces which makes them well suited for tasks such as border control, counterterrorism and public order functions in international peace operations.

On the other hand, it can also be argued that with regard to most of the tasks mentioned above the formal military status of gendarmeries in itself does not seem to provide any significant advantage, and these challenges might just as well be addressed by civilian police forces as long as they have, for example, the same heavy equipment or a similarly centralized structure. Indeed, in countries which do not have police forces with a military status, this is typically the case. The US Border Patrol, for example, responsible for controlling the country's borders, is a relatively centralized police force with a considerable amount of military-style equipment, yet it does not have a formal military status. This lack of a military status as such does not seem to hamper the Border Patrol's effectiveness. Similarly, special riot control or counterterrorist units without military status can be found in many countries, and the civilian nature of these forces does not seem to pose any significant disadvantage.[99] Thus, despite the significant roles gendarmerie-type forces play in the current security environment, their real added value seems to lie not so much in their formal military status *per se*, but rather in certain military characteristics in terms of organization and equipment – but these can also be found in purely civilian police forces.

The only notable exception to this, as far as European countries are concerned, seems to be in the area of international peace operations. Although this issue requires further research, a number of analysts have argued that the hybrid nature and formal military status of gendarmerie-type forces offer unique advantages that cannot be matched by purely civilian police forces.[100] This comparative advantage over civilian police relates in particular to the fact that gendarmeries may be deployed under both civilian and military command, they are used to working in tandem with military forces and most have at least some military training, none of which can be said of police forces with a civilian status. Moreover, as a result of their military status, gendarmeries are also more rapidly and more easily deployable in external operations than is typically the case for civilian police. It is also in this – and only in this – area where analysts have advocated the creation of gendarmerie-type forces in countries such as the USA, which traditionally do not have such agencies.[101]

Moreover, beyond the European context, it can be argued that in countries such as Algeria and Turkey, which have faced quasi-military internal challenges in the form of large-scale rebellions against the regime, the military status of gendarmerie forces seems to give a clear strategic advantage. As counterinsurgency operations are typically carried out under overall command of the armed forces, and gendarmerie units are deployed alongside the military, it arguably makes sense that the gendarmerie is closely integrated into the military command structure.

In addition, as mentioned at the outset of this paper, the military status of the gendarmerie has to be seen in the larger context of the dual police system, which in itself has certain advantages. The dual police model, as highlighted above, can be viewed as a mechanism of "checks and balances" within the internal security system, and the dissolution and merger of the gendarmerie with the police might thus bear the danger of an overcentralization of police power. Clearly this is an aspect which policy-makers would need to consider when contemplating the demilitarization and eventual fusion of the gendarmerie with the police. A more in-depth analysis of the cases of Austria and Belgium would likely provide valuable guidance in this regard.

Finally, how serious is the critique sometimes advanced against gendarmeries, namely that with their military status they represent a threat to civil liberties and human rights? While this question would require further research as well, at least prima facie evidence suggests that gendarmeries are not necessarily more likely than civilian police forces to commit abuses, and therefore do not as such represent a greater threat to individual freedoms. While human rights violations and other abuses have of course been committed in all regions discussed in this paper, there is no reason to believe that these have been related to the military status of the gendarmeries *per se*. To return to the example of border control, while there is evidence of human rights violations committed against irregular migrants by gendarmerie-type border control forces in several European countries, the same can be said of the US Border Control, which is an entirely civilian agency.[102]

Looking ahead

Given the trajectories of current developments, and the ambiguous value added of gendarmerie-type forces, how, then, are such agencies likely to evolve in the years to come? Given the long-term historical trend towards the demilitarization of internal security, the logical end-point of these developments seems to be the abolition of the formal military status of these police forces. To be sure, this might be a rather long-term development, as in countries such as France or Italy (although less so in Spain) the military status of the gendarmerie appears to retain broad-based legitimacy. This may be even more the case in the countries of the Maghreb and Turkey where, despite recent modest steps towards the demilitarization of the gendarmeries, their formal military status is unlikely to change in the foreseeable future.

However, as suggested by the experiences of Austria and Belgium, once the formal military status of the gendarmerie has been removed, the most likely outcome is that dissolution will eventually follow, with these forces being merged with the civilian police. Yet if both cases of dissolution in

Europe validate this trend, they also demonstrate that timeframes can vary widely.

While the longer-term prospects for gendarmeries as police forces with military status operating within the domestic sphere and on national territory may thus seem rather bleak, it can, however, also be assumed that such agencies will maintain or even enhance their role in the context of international peace operations. Not only is this the only area where gendarmeries can be said to have a decisive advantage as a result of their formal military status, but it is also a role which should be less affected by the general trend towards the demilitarization of internal security, as it is after all an external function from the point of view of the state providing assistance. A likely development, from this perspective, would thus be a split between two types of gendarmerie forces: one type would operate on the national territory, but would eventually be fully demilitarized and probably integrated into the civilian police; while the second type would be specifically intended for external operations and would retain its military status. Within the European context, EUROGENDFOR might foreshadow such a development, which could ultimately even lead to the creation of a permanent multinational gendarmerie force that would no longer be based on any one country and instead focus exclusively on international missions.

NOTES

[1] Albrecht Schnabel and Marc Krupanski, "Mapping Evolving Internal Roles of the Armed Forces", SSR Paper 7, Geneva Centre for the Democratic Control of Armed Forces, Geneva, 2012; Marleen Easton, Monica den Boer, Jelle Janssens, René Moelker and Tom Vander Beken (eds), *Blurring Military and Police Roles* (The Hague: Eleven International Publishing, 2010); Didier Bigo, "When Two Become One: Internal and External Securitisations in Europe", in Morten Kelstrup and Michael C. Williams (eds), *International Relations Theory and the Politics of European Integration: Power, Security and Community* (London: Routledge, 2000, pp. 171–205); Derek Lutterbeck, "Wearing the Outside In: Internal Deployment of the Armed Forces in Germany and Italy", *Sicherheit und Frieden*, 28(2), 2010, pp. 88–94.

[2] Derek Lutterbeck, "Between Police and Military: The New Security Agenda and the Rise of Gendarmeries", *Cooperation and Conflict*, 39(1), 2004, pp. 45–68. See also Hans Hovens and Gemma van Elk (eds), *Gendarmeries and the Security Challenges of the 21st Century* (The Hague: Koninklijke Marechaussee, 2011), www.fiep.org/wp-content/uploads/2011/11/FIEP-Seminarboek-totaal.pdf.

[3] See e.g. Andrew Scobell and Brad Hammit, "Goons, Gunmen, and Gendarmerie: Towards a Reconceptualisation of Paramilitary Formations", *Journal of Political and Military Sociology*, 26(2), 1998, pp. 213–232.

[4] See e.g. John Andrade, *World Police & Paramilitary Forces* (New York: Stockton Press, 1985, p. xi); David H. Bayley, *Patterns of Policing: A Comparative International Analysis* (New Brunswick, NJ: Rutgers University Press, 1985, p. 41).

[5] For a general overview of the adoption of the French police model in its African colonies see Organisation Internationale de la Francophonie, *La reforme des systèmes de sécurité et de justice en Afrique francophone* (Paris: Organisation Internationale de la Francophonie, 2010).

[6] Clive Emsley, "Peasants, Gendarmes and State Formation", in Mary Fulbrook (ed.) *National Histories and European History* (London: UCL Press, 1993, pp. 69–93).

[7] Bayley, note 4 above, p. 46; Rob Mawby, "Approaches to Comparative Analysis: The Impossibility of Becoming an Expert Everywhere", in Rob Mawby (ed.) *Policing Across the World: Issues for the Twenty-first Century* (London: UCL Press, 1999, pp. 13–22); P. A. J. Waddington, "Armed and Unarmed Policing", in Rob Mawby (ed.) *Policing Across the World: Issues for the Twenty-first Century* (London: UCL Press, 1999, pp. 151–166).

[8] The website of EuroCOP can be accessed at www.eurocop.org/.

[9] See e.g. Élisabeth Guigou, Alain Richard, Hubert Haenel, Renaud Denoix de Saint Marc, Pierre Truche and Hubert Blanc, *La Gendarmerie Nationale: Une institution républicaine au service du citoyen* (Paris: Editions Odile Jacob, 2000).

[10] Ibid., pp. 21–58.

[11] Ibid., pp. 59–104.

[12] Cross-country data on the manpower of police forces, comparable to, for example, the IISS publication *Military Balance*, are not published on a regular basis. International Institute for Strategic Studies, *Military Balance* (London: IISS, annual).

13   Calculated on the basis of Cour des comptes, "Les effectifs de l'Etat 1980–2008 – Un état des lieux", Cour des comptes, Paris, December 2009, www.ccomptes.fr/content/download/1318/12964/version/2/file/Rapport-effectifs-JO.pdf; Ministère de la Réforme de l'État, de la Décentralisation et de la Fonction Publique, "Rapport sur l'état de la fonction publique et les rémunérations", 2012, www.fonction-publique.gouv.fr/files/files/statistiques/jaunes/jaune2012_FP.pdf.

14   Information provided by Austrian Interior Ministry.

15   Information provided by Spanish Interior Ministry.

16   Lutterbeck, note 2 above, p. 53.

17   Ibid., p. 55.

18   Ibid., p. 56.

19   Alice Hills, "Border Control Services and Security Sector Reform", DCAF Working Paper No. 37, Geneva Centre for the Democratic Control of Armed Forces, Geneva, 2002, p. 12.

20   Derek Lutterbeck, "Policing Migration in the Mediterranean", *Mediterranean Politics*, 11(1), 2006, pp. 66–67; Wikipedia: "Servicio Marítimo de la Guardia Civil", http://es.wikipedia.org/wiki/Servicio_Mar%C3%ADtimo_de_la_Guardia_Civil.

21   Assemblée Nationale, Question No. 50888, 2 June 2009, http://questions.assemblee-nationale.fr/q13/13-50888QE.htm.

22   Wikipedia, "GSG 9", http://en.wikipedia.org/wiki/GSG_9.

23   Doppeladler.com, "EKO Cobra", www.doppeladler.com/misc/cobra.htm.

24   Lutterbeck, note 1 above.

25   See e.g. Manuel Castells, *The Power of Identity. The Information Age: Economy, Society and Culture*, Vol. II (Cambridge, MA and Oxford: Blackwell Publishers, 1997, pp. 68–107); Mark Irving Lichbach, "The Anti-Globalization Movement: A New Kind of Protest", in Monty G. Marshall and Ted Robert Gurr, *Peace and Conflict 2003: A Global Survey of Armed Conflicts, Self-Determination Movements, and Democracy* (College Park, MD: University of Maryland, 2003, pp. 39–42).

26   Patick Bruneteaux, *Maintenir l'Ordre* (Paris: Presse de la Fondation Nationale de Sciences Politiques, 1996).

27   Michiel de Weger, *The Potential of the European Gendarmerie Force* (The Hague: The Netherlands Institute of International Relations Clingendael, 2009); Annika S. Hansen, *From Congo to Kosovo: Civilian Police in Peace Operations*, Adelphi Paper 343 (London: Oxford University Press for IISS, 2002, pp. 71–72); Alice Hills, "The Inherent Limits of Military Forces in Policing Peace Operations", *International Peacekeeping*, 8, pp. 86–91.

28   See the EUROGENDFOR website at www.eurogendfor.org/. In 2009 Romania joined as well.

29   François Dieu, "Les missions de défense de la Gendarmerie", *Défense nationale*, 11, 2001, pp. 185–187. In the event of a war the Gendarmerie would be reinforced with its reserve units, numbering some 25,000 personnel.

30   In recent years 300–400 Gendarmerie officers have participated in international peace operations at any one point in time.

31   "Décret n° 2002-889 du 15 mai 2002 relatif aux attributions du ministre de l'intérieur, de la sécurité intérieure et des libertés locales", www.legifrance.gouv.fr/affichTexte.do?cidTexte=JORFTEXT000000596066&dateTexte=&categorieLien=id.

32   "Loi d'orientation et de programmation pour la sécurité intérieure", 29 August 2002.

[33] Ministère de l'Intérieure, "Circulaire du 22 mai 2002: Mise en place de groupes d'intervention régionaux", 22 May 2002.

[34] Sénat, "Quel avenir pour la gendarmerie?", Rapport d'Information No. 271, fait au nom de la commission des affaires étrangères, 10 April 2008, p. 38.

[35] "Loi n° 2009-971 du 3 août 2009 relative à la gendarmerie nationale", 3 August 2009.

[36] Sénat, "Rapport n° 66 (2008–2009) de M. Jean Faure, fait au nom de la commission des affaires étrangères, de la défense et des forces armées", 29 October 2008.

[37] "Charte du Gendarme", August 2009, printed in *Revue de la Gendarmerie Nationale*, 233, December 2009, pp. 31–36.

[38] Nicola Conforti, "The Italian Carabinieri: Old Traditions for a Modern Vision", in Hovens and van Elk, note 2 above, p. 233.

[39] Stefano Vespa, "Maroni studia come spostare i carabinieri dalla Difesa al Viminale", *Panorama*, 1 September 2009.

[40] Consiglio Centrale di Rappresentanza, Sezione CO.CE.R Carabinieri, "Razionalizzaione delle Forze di Polizia e Istituzione delle Ronde", 1 March 2009.

[41] Consiglio Centrale di Rappresentanza dell'Arma dei Carabinieri, "Carabinieri: COCER chiede la smilitarizzazione dell'Arma, 'noi citadini B'. Consensi e polemiche", press release, 15 March 2012.

[42] The only exception to this rule in the last 20 years has been General Carlos Gómez Arruche, who was nominated to this post by José Luis Rodríguez Zapatero's socialist government in 2004 despite its declared intention to demilitarize the Guardia Civil.

[43] The respective areas of responsibility are regulated in Organic Law 2/86 of 13 March 1986, Article 12.1.

[44] Partido Socialista Obrero Español, "Merecemos una España major. Programa Electoral Elecciones Generales 2004", PSOE, 2004, pp. 49–50, www.psoe.es/source-media/000000348500/000000348570.pdf.

[45] The website of the AUGC can be accessed at www.augc.org/. Notably, the AUGC is the only gendarmerie association which is a member of EuroCOP, one of whose main missions, as mentioned, is to advocate for the demilitarization of police forces in Europe.

[46] Associacion Unificada de Guardia Civiles, "XX Demandas para la modernizacion de le Guardia Civil", press release, 26 July 2005, www.psoe.es/izquierdasocialista/docs/57474/page/veinte-demandas-para-modernizacion-la-guardia-civil-.html.

[47] *El Confidencial Digital*, "Unificación de Policía Nacional y Guardia Civil. Las asociaciones mayoritarias (AUGC y SUP) ultiman un informe a favor: Se ahorraría el 35% del presupuesto de Interior", *El Confidencial Digital*, 5 August 2012.

[48] Bundesministerium für Inneres, *Die Gendarmerie in Österreich* (Vienna: BMI, 1989, p. 12).

[49] However, after the Second World War part of the Federal Gendarmerie served as a basis for the recreation of the Austrian armed forces. Ibid., pp. 15–27.

[50] Bundesministerium für Inneres, *Grenzdienst der Bundesgendarmerie* (Vienna: BMI, 1999).

[51] Austria Presse Agentur, "Ministerium: Forderung nach Zusammenlegung wie wenn der Dalai Lama die Katholische und Evangelische Kirche zusammenlegen will", Austria Presse Agentur, 8 April 2000 (author's translation).

[52] *Öffentliche Sicherheit*, "Gewinn an Sicherheit", *Öffentliche Sicherheit*, 12A/05, pp. 6–12.

53 Bernadette Keusch, "Drei gegen die Macht der Minister", *Der Standard*, 19 September 2009.

54 Lode van Outrive, Yves Cartuyvels and Paul Ponsaers, *Les Polices en Belgique: Histoire socio-politique du systéme policier de 1794 à nos jours* (Brussels: Vie Ouvrière, 1991, pp. 307–314).

55 Ibid., p. 315.

56 Maurice Punch, "Rotten Orchards: 'Pestilence', Police Misconduct and System Failure", *Policing and Society*, 13(2), 2003, pp. 171–196; Denis Bergmans, "Police and Gendarmerie Reform in Belgium", in Ümit Cizre and Ibrahim Cerrah (eds), *Security Sector Governance: Turkey and Europe*, DCAF-TESEV Series in Security Sector Studies No. 4 (Istanbul: DCAF/TESEV, 2008, pp. 101–115).

57 Morris Janowitz, *Military Institutions and Coercion in the Developing Nations* (Chicago, IL: University of Chicago Press, 1977).

58 Ibid., pp. 44–47.

59 Sunil Dasgupta, "Understanding Paramilitary Growth: Agency Relations in Military Organisation", paper presented at conference on "Curbing human rights violations by non-state armed groups", Centre of International Relations, Liu Institute for Global Issues, University of British Colombia, Vancouver, 13–15 November 2003.

60 In Turkey, the French police model was imported in the nineteenth century by French police advisers.

61 The figure of 130,000 was reportedly mentioned by a representative of the Gendarmerie in 2012. See Kaci Haider, "La Gendarmerie se renforce par six unités aériennes", *Algérie 1*, 9 July 2012. The country profile by the US Library of Congress gives the figure of 60,000 (for 2008), whereas *Military Balance*, note 12 above, reports a mere 20,000 men for the Gendarmerie.

62 The conflict erupted after the Algerian government cancelled the 1991 legislative elections, the first round of which was won by Islamist parties.

63 Luis Martinez, *La guerre civile en Algérie 1990–1998* (Paris: Editions Karthala, 1998, p. 232).

64 Ibid.; Anthony Cordesman, *A Tragedy of Arms: Military and Security Developments in the Maghreb* (Westport, CT: Praeger, 2002, p. 160); Bruno Callies de Salies, "Les luttes de clan exacerbent la guerre civile", *Le Monde diplomatique*, October 1997.

65 *Le Soir d'Algérie*, "Trois unités d'élite on evité le pire à Tiguentourine: Le GIS, la DSI et les commandos parachutistes, la force de frappe de l'ANP", *Le Soir d'Algérie*, 10 January 2013.

66 Steven A. Cook, *Ruling But Not Governing: The Military and Political Development in Egypt, Algeria and Turkey* (Baltimore, MD: Johns Hopkins University Press, 2007, pp. 32–62).

67 Ali Idir, "La police et la gendarmerie placés sous commandement de l'armée", *Tout sur l'Algérie*, 4 July 2011.

68 Driss Bennani and Mohammed Boudarham, "Gendarmerie royale: L'armée à tout faire", *Telquel*, 19 August 2012.

69 Hanspeter Mattes, "Morocco: Reforms in the Security Sector But No 'SSR'", in Hans Born and Albrecht Schnabel (eds), *Security Sector Reform in Challenging Environments* (Münster: LIT Verlag, 2009, p. 154).

70   Ibid.

71   The relationship between the Moroccan armed forces and the Gendarmerie is described in a US diplomatic cable leaked by Wikileaks: US Embassy Rabat, "Morocco's Military: Adequate, Modernizing, But Facing Big Challenges", 4 August 2008 (ID: 164775).

72   Instead of a minister of defence, Morocco has a minister delegate for the administration of national defence.

73   Lewis B. Ware, "The Role of the Tunisian Military in the Post-Bourguiba Era", *Middle East Journal*, 39(1), 1985, p. 37; Lewis B. Ware, *Tunisia in the Post-Bourguiba Era: The Role of the Military in a Civil Arab Republic* (Montgomery, AL: Air University Press, 1986, p. 47).

74   Michel Camau and Vincent Geisser, *Le syndrome autoritaire. Politique en Tunisie de Bourguiba à Ben Ali* (Paris: Presses de Sciences Politiques, 2003, p. 211).

75   "Décret no. 2006-1162 du 13 avril 2006 portant sur le statut particulier de corps de la garde nationale (article 2)."

76   Among the reasons why so many protesters died during the anti-regime uprising in late 2010 and early 2011 was the fact that many National Guard and police units were equipped with military rifles, so even if demonstrators were shot "only" in the legs, ricocheting bullets would kill several persons. See Abdelaziz Belkhodja and Tarak Cheikhrouhou, *14 janvier: L'enquête* (Tunis: Appolina Editions, 2013, pp. 30–33).

77   Even though in principle Tunisian police officers could claim compensation for overtime work, in practice this was negligible.

78   Tahar Ben Youssef, *Les snipers dans la révolution tunisienne et la réforme du système sécuritaire* (Tunis: Tahar Ben Youssef, 2011, pp. 106–116).

79   Derek Lutterbeck, "After the Fall: Security Sector Reform in post-Ben Ali Tunisia", Arab Reform Initiative, October 2012, p. 19, www.arab-reform.net/after-fall-security-sector-reform-post-ben-ali-tunisia.

80   *Espace Manager*, "Tunisie – La fusion de la police et de la Garde nationale en question", *Espace Manager*, 19 November 2012.

81   See Ümit Cizre (ed.), *Almanac Turkey 2005: Security Sector and Democratic Oversight*, DCAF-TESEV Series in Security Sector Studies (Istanbul and Geneva: TESEV/DCAF, 2006, pp. 100–111).

82   Again, there are conflicting reports on the size of the Turkish Gendarmerie. While *Military Balance*, note 12 above, cites 150,000 men, official Turkish sources provide a figure of 205,103. See Anahtar Kelimeler, "İşte TSK'nın personel sayısı!", *Haber Turk*, 1 February 2012.

83   Henri J. Barkey and Graham E. Fuller, *Turkey's Kurdish Question* (Lanham, MD: Rowman & Littlefield, 1998, pp. 133–155); Amnesty International, "Turkey: No Security without Human Rights", Amnesty International, London, October 1996; US Department of State, "Turkey: Country Report on Human Rights Practices – 1999", US Department of State, Washington, DC, 23 February 2000.

84   Norwegian Refugee Council/Global IDP Project, "Profile of Internal Displacement Turkey", Norwegian Refugee Council and Global IDP Project, Geneva, October 2005, pp. 31–33, www.internal-displacement.org/8025708F004BE3B1/(httpInfoFiles)/A0D784C01 4878D59802570BA00568E64/$file/Turkey%20-October%202005.pdf.

85 Alper Bilgic, "The Turkish Gendarmerie: A Source of Honour", in Hovens and van Elk, note 2 above, p. 244.

86 See e.g. Lale Sarıibrahimoğlu, "Gendarmerie", in Ümit Cizre (ed.), *Democratic Oversight and Reform of the Security Sector in Turkey* (Münster: LIT Verlag, 2008, pp. 141–158); Ümit Cizre, "The Catalysts, Directions and Focus of Turkey's Agenda for Security Sector Reform in the 21st Century", DCAF Working Paper No. 148, Geneva Centre for the Democratic Control of Armed Forces, Geneva, August 2004, pp. 20–21; Biriz Berksoy, "Military, Police and Intelligence in Turkey: Recent Transformations and Needs for Reform", Policy Report Series, TESEV Democratisation Programme, Istanbul, June 2013, pp. 22–25.

87 Sarıibrahimoğlu, ibid., p. 145.

88 In practically all the EU's "progress reports" on Turkey's accession, the strengthening of civilian control over the Gendarmerie is mentioned.

89 Sedat Güneç, "Turkish Gendarmerie to Meet European Standards", *Today's Zaman*, 10 November 2008.

90 Ercan Yavuz, "EU Reform in Gendarmerie Force Remains Stalled", *Today's Zaman*, 16 November 2010.

91 Berksoy, note 86 above, p. 23.

92 Fatma Disli Zibak, "New EMASYA-like Protocol Involves Military in Domestic Security", *Today's Zaman*, 28 June 2013.

93 According to Berksoy, the abolition of the previous EMASYA protocol did not significantly change the military's propensity to launch internal security missions without consent of the civilian authorities. See Berksoy, note 86 above, p. 23.

94 The only other example in the European context is the German Federal Border Police (Bundesgrenzschutz), whose military status was also removed in the 1970s but which still exists today in the form of the Federal Police (Bundespolizei). The Federal Border Police's military status was, however, closely related to the post-Second World War division of Germany and the tensions along the inner German border. Moreover, the German police system is different from that of other countries with gendarmeries, in that the competence to set up police forces lies mainly with the *Länder* and not the federal state.

95 As mentioned, "demilitarization" is understood here mainly in institutional terms. A more in-depth analysis of this process would need to take into account other dimensions as well, including for example "military culture". It might very well be that despite the (formal) dissolution of the gendarmeries in Austria and Belgium, a "military mindset" persists within the unified (civilian) police forces which took their place.

96 Anthony Giddens, *The Nation-State and Violence* (Berkeley, CA and Los Angeles, CA: University of California Press, 1987, pp. 181–192); Christopher Dandeker, *Surveillance, Power and Modernity* (Cambridge: Polity Press, 1990, p. 58).

97 Another reversal of this trend can seen in the increasing use by police and law enforcement agencies of military-style technology (such as heavy weaponry, night-vision devices, etc.), which has been described (and criticized) by many analysts as the "militarization of policing". See e.g. Peter B. Kraska (ed.), *Militarizing the American Criminal Justice System* (Boston, MA: Northeastern University Press, 2001); Derek Lutterbeck, "Blurring the Dividing Line: The Convergence of Internal and External

Security in Western Europe", *European Security*, 14(2), 2005, pp. 231–253. It could be argued that the long-term historical trend is towards reducing the "overt" or visible presence of the military in internal security provision, while military influence might persist or even increase in more "covert" or subtle forms (such as the use of military technology by internal security forces).

[98] Schnabel and Krupanski, note 1 above; Lutterbeck, note 1 above.

[99] Indeed, in France in recent years it has increasingly been the (civilian) National Police, and in particular its Compagnies Républicaines de Sécurité, which has taken over the task of riot control from the Gendarmerie mobile.

[100] Cornelius Friesendorf, "International Intervention and the Use of Force: Military and Police Roles", SSR Paper No. 4, Geneva Centre for the Democratic Control of Armed Forces, Geneva, 2012, p. 79.

[101] See e.g. David T. Armitage Jr and Anne M. Moisan, "Constabulary Forces and Postconflict Transition: The Euro-Atlantic Dimension", Strategic Forum 218, Institute for National Strategic Studies, National Defense University, Washington, DC, November 2005.

[102] See e.g. European Union Agency for Fundamental Rights, *Fundamental Rights at Europe's Southern Sea Borders* (Luxembourg: Publications Office of the European Union, 2013); Timothy J. Dunn, *The Militarization of the U.S.-Mexico Border, 1978–1992: Low-Intensity Conflict Doctrine Comes Home* (Austin, TX: University of Texas Press, 1995).

www.ingramcontent.com/pod-product-compliance
Lightning Source LLC
Chambersburg PA
CBHW080502030726
47592CB00011B/3211